Circle
of Influence

*Implementing Shared
Decision Making and
Participative Management*

Paula Jorde Bloom

NEW HORIZONS

EDUCATIONAL CONSULTANTS AND LEARNING RESOURCES

LAKE FOREST, ILLINOIS 60045-0863

Publisher's Cataloging-in-Publication

Bloom, Paula J.
     Circle of influence : implementing shared
decision making and participative management /
Paula Jorde Bloom — 1st ed.
     p. cm. — (The Director's toolbox : a
management series for early childhood
administrators)
     Includes bibliographical references.
     LCCN: 99-68480
     ISBN: 0-9621894-3-X

     1. Day care centers—United States—
Administration. 2. Group decision making.
3. Management—Employee participation.   I. Title

HV854.J67 2000   362.71'2'068
                          QBI99-1893

NEW HORIZONS

Educational Consultants and Learning Resources
P.O. Box 863
Lake Forest, Illinois 60045-0863
(847) 295-8131
(847) 295-2968 FAX

Books in The Director's Toolbox Management Series are
available at quantity discounts for use in training programs.
For information on bulk quantity rates or how to purchase a
Trainer's Guide for this book, contact the publisher.

Illustrations – *Loel Barr*
Design – *Stan Burkat*

CONTENTS

Chapter

About the Author

Paula Jorde Bloom holds a joint appointment as Director of the Center for Early Childhood Leadership and Professor of Early Childhood Education at National-Louis University in Wheeling, Illinois. She received her baccalaureate degree from Southern Connecticut State University and her master's and Ph.D. degrees from Stanford University. Paula has taught preschool and kindergarten, designed and directed a child care center, and served as administrator of a campus laboratory school. She is a frequent keynote speaker at state, national, and international early childhood conferences and serves as consultant to professional organizations and state agencies. Dr. Bloom is the author of numerous articles and several widely read books including <u>Living and Learning with Children</u>, <u>Avoiding Burnout</u>, <u>A Great Place to Work</u>, and <u>Blueprint for Action</u>.

Acknowledgements

The stories that directors share in the management workshops I conduct have always served as a rich source of material for my writing. For this book, I am particularly indebted to Teri Talan, Phoebe Leopoldo, and Marcia Newsome for providing some wonderful examples of shared decision making in action. Thanks to Laura Lipton from Pathways to Understanding for sharing some of the consensus building strategies included in these pages. I am grateful to my colleagues at the Center for Early Childhood Leadership—Eileen Eisenberg, Donna Rafanello, Joan Britz, Janis Jones, Lila Goldston, and Tim Walker—for the real-life lessons they have taught me about participative management. Finally, I extend special thanks to Heather Knapp for her assistance in tracking down the original source of the quotes and cartoons and to Catherine Cauman and Donna Rafanello for their careful editing of the manuscript.

CHAPTER 1

Introduction

Although it took place more than twenty years ago, I can recall with clarity my first staff meeting as the director of a new child care center. I had read several articles extolling the virtues of participative management and was determined to develop a spirit of shared decision making and collaboration at my center. I carefully orchestrated the details leading up to this meeting. I invited several teachers to contribute ideas for the meeting agenda and reminded everyone about the meeting time. Ever mindful of the importance of ambiance, I arranged the chairs in a circle, put fresh flowers on the table, and brought in home-baked cookies. Finally, I made sure telephone calls would be intercepted to minimize distractions.

During the meeting everyone was polite and respectful, but they clearly were not deeply invested in the discussion. It lacked spirit; it seemed flat. I thought perhaps people were tired after a long day of work and made a mental note to bring chocolate to our next meeting. We adjourned.

Afterward, as I was cleaning up the room, I happened to look out the window. There in the parking lot, the *real* staff meeting was taking place. The teachers were engaged in animated discussion about all the subjects on our agenda. I scratched my head in puzzlement. Where had I gone wrong?

Thus my first lesson in participative management: collaboration does not come easily. I suspect my experience is not unique. Reading about and understanding the principles of participative management are far easier than putting those principles into practice. While I no longer direct a center, I work closely with directors who still struggle with these issues daily. I am convinced that participative management is essential for high-quality program functioning. I am also convinced that implementing it is a complicated and sometimes messy process.

I've come a long way in understanding the dynamics of organizational life since that first staff meeting. I've learned that trust is essential to participative management and that trust must be nurtured over time. It takes patience, persistence, and above all a genuine willingness to seriously consider differing points of view.

You as director are in a unique position to influence the decision-making policies and practices at your center. You have access to more information than your teachers do because you monitor all aspects of your center's operations. You probably also set agendas for staff meetings, deciding which topics will be discussed and which decisions will be made and when. In sum, you have a repertoire of tactics you can employ to keep your authority and influence centralized, thereby discouraging teachers' active involvement in substantive issues.

You are also in a position, however, to do otherwise—to implement management strategies that empower your staff and make them vital partners in achieving centerwide goals.

In this book you'll learn that participative management is both a philosophy and a set of behaviors that define your interactions with people. You'll explore techniques for managing the daily business of your center by involving others in critical decisions affecting their job satisfaction and professional fulfillment. If you implement these strategies and expand your staff's circle of influence, you can reap the benefits of true collaboration and commitment to shared goals.

Before we plunge into the rationale behind shared decision making and the strategies to make it happen, take a few moments to think about your own situation. Complete the following exercises.

exercise 1

List two decisions you made last week in your role as director and indicate whom these decisions affect.

Decision	*Who is affected*
_____	_____
_____	_____

exercise 2

Describe a situation in which you made a decision with good intentions that was later misinterpreted by one or several teachers.

_____

_____

_____

_____

On a scale of 0 to 100 (no influence at all to a great deal of influence), how do you believe your staff would rate

- their current degree of decision-making influence _____

- their desired degree of decision-making influence _____

CHAPTER 2

What Is Participative Management, and Why Is It Important?

Participative management goes by many names—Total Quality Management (TQM), democratic leadership, open-book management, Theory Z, quality circles, re-engineering, and site-based management. Whatever its formal title, this approach involves democratic leadership and shared decision making as central tenets. When carried out in good faith, participative management can yield such benefits as improved employee morale, increased job satisfaction, and deeper staff commitment to the organization.

Three Principles of Collaboration

Organizations as entities do not have values. Rather, the values that guide organizations come from the individuals who set up their structures and carry out their various business processes. In most child care settings, that individual is you the director.

In collaborative organizations, three fundamental assumptions guide the participative management.

- **The whole is greater than the sum of its parts.** Any section of an orchestra can produce music, but how much more powerful is the music when all parts—strings, woodwinds, percussion, brass—work together. Participative management is based on the belief that when more people participate, a synergistic effect increases the possibility of better decisions.

- **People have a right to be involved in making decisions that affect their lives.** From a human relations perspective, this second principle makes good sense. Research supports the proposition that when teachers are given the opportunity to participate in making decisions that affect them, they experience greater job satisfaction and higher morale. They also tend to hold a higher opinion of their supervisors.

- **People involved in making decisions have a greater stake in carrying out those decisions than do individuals who are not involved.** Effective leaders know that how decisions are made can have a more lasting impact on people's attitudes about work than the decision itself. People remember the process, the way they were consulted (or not consulted), longer than they remember the details of the decision. Put simply, when staff participate meaningfully in making a decision, they more fully understand that decision. Thus, they are more likely to work for successful implementation of the decision than to sabotage it.

Different Roles Lead to Different Perceptions

While many agree about the importance of participation and shared ownership, fewer agree on their meaning. In most early childhood work environments, meaningful participation remains an elusive construct because the definition of meaningful participation is based on subjective perceptions.

A director who has worked her way up through the ranks from classroom teacher understands that people holding different positions in the organizational hierarchy view decision-making processes differently. Directors consistently tend to view their programs more positively than do the teachers.

Take a look at the graph below. It compares the perceptions of directors and teachers on ten dimensions of organizational climate. In all ten areas directors tend to have more positive perceptions of organizational practices than do teachers.

**A Comparison of Directors' and Teachers' Perceptions
of the Organizational Climate of Their Centers**

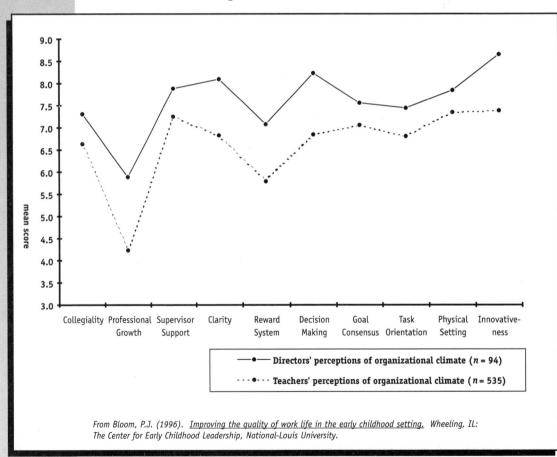

From Bloom, P.J. (1996). _Improving the quality of work life in the early childhood setting._ Wheeling, IL: The Center for Early Childhood Leadership, National-Louis University.

I believe the situation can be distilled to a simple axiom of organizational life: _Teachers and directors often have very different perceptions of what is going on in a center._ Although teachers and directors may generally agree on which problems are serious, they can differ considerably in their perceptions of the magnitude of those problems. Differing perceptions can get in the way of genuine collaboration.

Why the difference in perceptions? Several complex and interrelated factors may be at work, including differences in the backgrounds of directors and teachers, the scope and nature of their roles, and the perceived control directors and teachers have over their jobs. The decision-making structure of a program may look quite egalitarian on paper; in reality, however, teachers perceive a strong hierarchical arrangement.

In a study of 2,161 teachers and 541 directors in 36 states, respondents were asked whether they agreed with eight statements about decision making at their centers. The findings show that directors genuinely believe they provide ample opportunity for staff involvement in critical issues affecting their professional well-being; teachers, on the other hand, have a different view of organizational life. The following graph summarizes these data.

Agreement with Statements About Decision Making: A Comparison of Directors' and Teachers' Responses

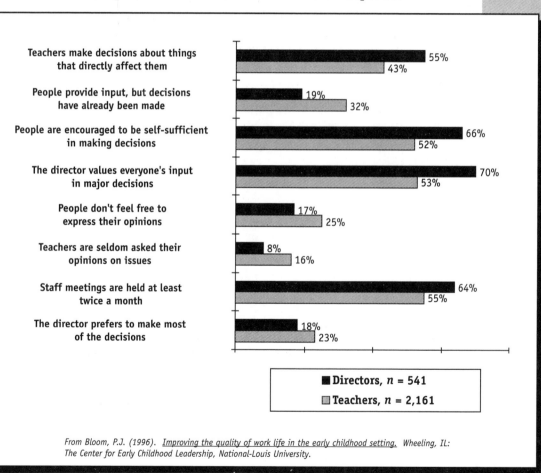

Statement	Directors	Teachers
Teachers make decisions about things that directly affect them	55%	43%
People provide input, but decisions have already been made	19%	32%
People are encouraged to be self-sufficient in making decisions	66%	52%
The director values everyone's input in major decisions	70%	53%
People don't feel free to express their opinions	17%	25%
Teachers are seldom asked their opinions on issues	8%	16%
Staff meetings are held at least twice a month	64%	55%
The director prefers to make most of the decisions	18%	23%

■ Directors, n = 541
▨ Teachers, n = 2,161

From Bloom, P.J. (1996). *Improving the quality of work life in the early childhood setting.* Wheeling, IL: The Center for Early Childhood Leadership, National-Louis University.

Teachers may not always be aware of the consideration that the director gives their views and the competing factors the director must consider when making decisions. Nevertheless, perceptions are powerful regulators of behavior that can influence teachers' level of commitment to a center. In fact, people's perceptions of events may be more important than reality because individuals act according to their interpretations of events. Directors need to be alert to the possibility that teachers have different perceptions of the decision-making processes from their own.

The graph below compares teachers' perceptions of their current and desired levels of decision-making influence in five areas. Teachers were asked how much influence they currently had in each area and how much influence they would like to have. In all five areas, teachers indicated that they would like to have more influence.

A Comparison of Teachers' Perceptions of Their Current and Desired Decision-Making Influence

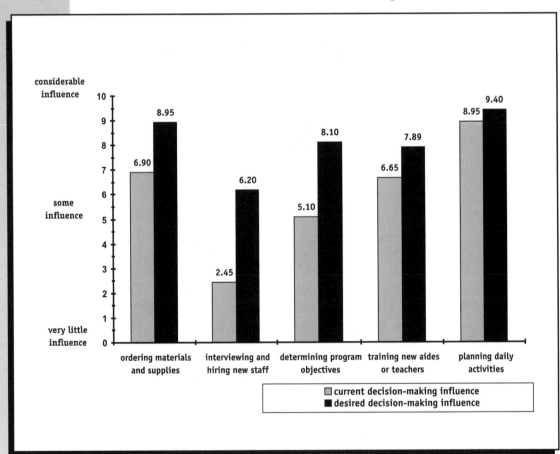

When these data are combined, they show that more than three-fourths of teachers reported having less decision-making influence than they would like. Less than one-fifth (16%) felt they had just the right amount, and only 6% indicated having too much decision-making responsibility. From these data we can conclude that in the area of decision making, there is considerable room for empowering teachers.

**Teachers' Perceptions of Their
Overall Decision-Making Influence**

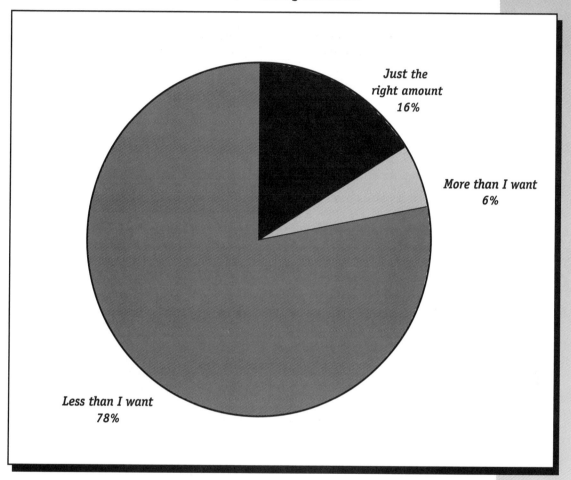

Rethinking Management Involves the Head and the Heart

Effective leadership is a function of both the head and the heart. Implementing a model of participative management requires a shift in both your head and your heart if are to succeed.

Intellectually it means shifting your problem-solving orientation from an **either/or mindset** to a **both/and mindset.** An either/or mindset handles decision making as a straightforward choice between competing alternatives, A or B, right or wrong, good or bad. While this approach may seem efficient, it often fosters competition and creates a climate of happy winners and disgruntled losers. Participative management requires a both/and mindset, one that encourages collaboration and strives to achieve win/win solutions to problems.

Problem-Solving Orientations

	Either/Or	Both/And
Value system	Competitive	Collaborative
Type of outcome expected	Win/lose	Win/win
Attitude toward "winning"	To the victor go the spoils	Your success is my success
Attitude toward "losing"	Someone has to lose	If someone loses, everyone loses
Attitude toward minority opinions	Get with the program	Everyone holds a piece of the truth
Why explore differences between competing positions?	To search for bargaining chips in preparation for horsetrading and compromise	To build a shared framework of understanding in preparation for mutual creative thinking
Essential mental activity	Analyze: break the whole into parts	Synthesize: integrate parts into a whole
How long it takes	Faster in the short run	Faster in the long run
When to use	When expedience is more important than durability	When all parties have the power to block any decision and the issue is for high stakes
Underlying philosophy	Survival of the fittest	Interdependence of all things

From Kaner, S. (1996). _Facilitator's guide to participatory decision-making_ (p. 147). Gabriola Island, British Columbia: New Society Publishers. Reprinted with permission.

Implementing a model of participative management requires a heartfelt, sustained commitment to changing the interpersonal dynamics at your child care center and a willingness to muck through the mess of modifying organizational structures and processes. This means making a conscious effort to find ways to empower your staff and enhance their circle of influence in day-to-day decision making. It is not about adopting a singular way of thinking or problem solving, but rather about honoring diverse approaches and respecting multiple perspectives on the difficult issues that are the substance of your work in early care and education.

This no doubt means changing how individuals interact and accomplish things as well as changing the way roles are defined and practices implemented. To achieve success you must be genuinely committed to the principles of shared decision making because your efforts will take time and involve an element of risk.

If you are not sincere, your staff may perceive your attempts as manipulative. If you are genuinely interested in giving them a greater voice in a variety of decisions, however, you will be richly rewarded. In programs that have moved toward participative management, staff are more committed and professionally fulfilled. This results in higher levels of job satisfaction and lower turnover.

"I'm not sure—I'll have to take it up with my staff"

Drawing by Rex May. Reprinted with permission.

How a leader really behaves is less important than how members of his group perceive he behaves; it is their perception of his behavior that will determine the behavior of the group members, and will hence define the organizational climate.

A. Halpin and D. Croft

CHAPTER 3

The First Step – Looking Within

The move toward participative management begins with
thoughtful self-reflection—taking time to assess your beliefs about
power and influence, your decision-making style, and your work style.
The director must be able to create a climate where individuals can openly discuss
highly charged topics relating to power and control, how issues are decided, and
how work is carried out. This cannot happen without first reflecting on and
assessing values and beliefs about power and influence in the workplace.

How Do You Perceive Power?

Four metaphorical images can represent different management philosophies. As you
read their descriptions, think about your own management philosophy and
leadership style.

- **The Power Pie.** This management philosophy
  holds that in any organization, there is only so
  much power to go around. If you as director give
  away a slice of your power, you will have less power
  and others will have more. This is essentially a
  zero-sum philosophy of power—that power is a
  limited and scarce resource. It is also a management
  philosophy that can become a self-fulfilling
  prophecy. If individuals believe it, they will begin
  hoarding power; they will be reluctant to share information and involve
  others in making decisions.

- **The Balancing Scale.** The balancing scale is
  another image based on a management philosophy
  that power, control, and influence in the workplace
  are scarce commodities. If you give some of your
  power or decision-making authority to someone
  else, the balance of influence may tip toward that
  person. When decision making is based on the
  management philosophy that there is a finite
  amount of power to go around, organizations tend
  to promote practices that ensure that the "person in charge" maintains a
  competitive edge—that the scale is tipped in his or her direction.

These two metaphors for the distribution of power tend to support traditional models of hierarchical management where there is a clear chain of command and defined responsibilities. Such models often serve to limit power and influence at lower levels. They arise and are maintained for different reasons, some malevolent (egocentric needs of those with leadership roles), some benevolent (genuine desire of leadership to protect staff from the burdens of management).

One of the clearest examples of the power-scarcity mentality in hierarchical organizations is secrecy of information. Information is power; more information is increased power. Thus hoarding information or sharing only portions of it becomes the organizational norm.

Collaborative organizations, on the other hand, concentrate not on the elimination of power, but on its equalization and disbursement: Directors who use power in a positive way empower others. Two other metaphors capture this management philosophy.

- **Candles.** Imagine yourself in a dark room. If you light a candle, a soft glow permeates the room. Now imagine that the candle you hold symbolizes your power and influence as director of the center. If you use your candle to light a candle held by a teacher, thus sharing your power and influence, what happens to your candle? What happens to the glow in the darkroom? A management philosophy based on the candle metaphor promotes a power-abundance mentality. Not only is your candle not diminished when you light another, but the light in the room increases as well.

- **A flock of geese.** If you've ever watched a flock of migrating geese, you will have noticed the V formation that characterizes their aeronautical team effort. The V is purposeful because, as each bird flaps its wings, the flapping creates an uplift for the bird that follows. By flying in a V formation, the whole flock has a 71% greater flying range than does a bird flying solo. The lead goose assumes that position for a short distance only, then rotates back into the V, allowing a different goose to fly at the point. The geese in formation honk to encourage those up front to keep up their speed. When a goose falters, two or more other geese drop out of the formation and follow it down, helping and protecting the incapacitated goose until it can join another flock. The leadership lessons we can learn from our fine-feathered friends are powerful.

As you examine your belief system, ask yourself if you truly believe that your staff is comprised of creative, responsible individuals whose ideas and suggestions will enhance decision quality. If you don't genuinely believe that your teachers and support staff can contribute meaningfully to important centerwide decisions, you probably won't be willing to let go of some of the control and influence you currently enjoy and your staff will perceive your attempts at participative management as disingenuous.

The following summarizes the key values that administrators need to embrace if participative management is to succeed in an early childhood work environment.

Values That Support Participative Management

Directors believe that . . .

- teachers and support staff are responsible, motivated, and trustworthy and that each has something to contribute

- teachers and support staff have information, skills, and creative talents that, when shared, will increase decision quality

- open expression of ideas and feelings is healthy and suppression of thoughts and beliefs reduces the quality of decisions

- conflict is not something to be avoided, but is a potential source of information rather than a threat or challenge

- influence in the child care center should be based upon expertise rather than role designation

Adapted from Wood, C. J. (1984). Participatory decision making: Why doesn't it seem to work? Educational Forum, 49 (1), 59.

What is Your Decision-Making Style?

Take a few minutes to think about your current decision-making style by completing Exercise 4. An interpretation of your style will be provided in Chapter 4.

Think about the way you typically make decisions that have centerwide implications (for example, hiring a new teacher, expanding program options, adjusting program hours, modifying program philosophy, or planning a schoolwide social event). Read each of the statements below and choose **three** that are most typical for you for these types of decisions.

1. As director, I have the big picture of center operations, so I usually make most of the important decision pertaining to program operations.

2. I like to bring issues to my staff and get 100% agreement before we proceed.

3. I present my ideas to my staff and get their input before I make a final decision on most important issues.

4. I bring issues before my staff and take a vote. I implement the majority decision.

5. I defer to my staff's expertise and let them form a committee to decide on important issues.

6. I ask a few of my most experienced staff to make key decisions regarding the program.

7. I don't think it is necessary for everyone to agree 100% on a course of action, but I like to get general agreement from my staff on an issue before proceeding.

8. I weigh all the pros and cons of an issue, make a decision, and then "sell" it to my staff.

9. I make a tentative decision on an issue pertaining to the program and test the reactions of several teachers before making my final decision.

10. I don't want to burden my staff with extra work, so I typically make most centerwide decisions myself.

11. I appoint ad hoc committees for making different centerwide issues.

12. I set up an advisory group of teachers to provide feedback to me on different issues before I make my final decision.

What about Your Work Style

Self-reflection includes a careful examination of how work is done at your center, and particularly how you assign or delegate work to others. Think about your typical work behavior as a supervisor as you complete Exercise 5.

For each situation described below, select the response that best describes your typical behavior.

1. In a typical week

   a. I complete my work within 40 hours.
   b. I work 40 hours plus many evenings and weekends.

2. In a typical week I spend most of my time

   a. evaluating the program, training staff, and planning.
   b. answering the phone, attending meetings, and resolving personnel problems.

3. When I'm on vacation, my time off is

   a. only occasionally interrupted by center emergencies.
   b. frequently interrupted by calls about routine problems.

4. When I delegate a task to a staff member,

   a. I explain the result expected and allow the individual to "do her thing."
   b. I spell out how to complete the task, step by step.

5. After I've delegated a task,

   a. I have the individual provide periodic progress reports.
   b. I check once or twice a day to see how it's going.

6. When a staff member is floundering with a delegated task,

   a. I offer to provide whatever assistance is needed.
   b. I take the job back and do it myself.

7. When a staff member does an acceptable but not exceptional job on a delegated task,

   a. I accept the work and point out how it could be improved next time.
   b. I do it over myself.

8. When a staff member suggests a change in my way of doing a task,

   a. I assess the pros and cons of each approach.
   b. I become defensive and show why my way is best.

Reprinted with permission from Child Care Information Exchange, *P.O. Box 3249, Redmond, WA 98073, (800) 221-2864.*

If you answered these eight questions with more b's than a's, you may want to think about your inability to let go of control, your drive for perfection, or your reluctance to trust others to make wise and good decisions. How often do you find yourself thinking any of the following statements?

- "No one can do the job as well as I can."
- "No one can do it as fast as I can."
- "When I do it myself, I know it'll get done right."
- "No one has enough interest, knowledge, or skill to do the task."

Many directors are reluctant to delegate because they genuinely want to protect their staff from taking on more work than they need to, particularly given their low pay and compensation. The irony is that their desire to protect their staff from additional burdens may be having just the opposite effect—staff may interpret these protective behaviors as a lack of trust in their ability to perform tasks competently. This decreases motivation in the long run.

Getting work done through others is central to the director's leadership role. Good leaders, those who have refined the art of delegating, challenge staff with assignments that match their mental and physical capabilities. The benefits of delegating are multifold: it stretches people and provides job enrichment for staff; it makes them a more integral part of the center's operation; it builds a more unified team spirit; and it forces directors to be more organized. The bonus for the director is that when decision-making functions are shared, staff gain a greater appreciation for and insight into the dimensions of the administrative role.

I f you perform a task that someone else could do, you keep yourself from a task that only you could do.

CHAPTER 4

A Framework for Shared Decision Making

Why is it that so many well-intentioned efforts to implement a model of participative management fail—that teachers experience frustration rather than fulfillment? Efforts at shared decision making are often viewed by teachers as a formality or an attempt to create the illusion of teacher influence; they represent token changes at best. When teachers are involved, their participation is limited and sporadic. This is because most administrative efforts to share decision making often constitute procedural rather than real substantive changes.

The following framework is intended to help you determine when decision making can be expanded to include other stakeholders in key decisions affecting your center. It rests on the premise that the effectiveness of decisions is determined by both the quality of the decision and the acceptance and commitment of others in implementing the decision. The goal is to reduce the incidence of decision making by default and decisions that are not implemented, as well as reduce the frustration in interpersonal relations when the methods for making decisions are not understood. The following four questions provide the basis for implementing the framework:

- Who are the stakeholders?
- What are the different types of decisions?
- What are the possible levels of participation?
- What are the external constraints?

Who Are the Stakeholders?

In the management of early childhood programs, there are a number of potential stakeholders. These may include

- the board of directors
- the owner of the center
- the director or other key administrators
- teachers and assistant teachers
- support staff (cook, social workers, secretary)
- parents
- children
- community representatives

In general, the degree to which these stakeholders participate in decision making relates to the degree to which authority is centralized. As greater participation occurs, influence and power are dispersed and there tends to be a flattening in the hierarchical structure of the organization.

What Are the Different Types of Decisions?

Every day center directors are confronted with a bewildering array of decisions—some minor and perfunctory (scheduling school pictures) and some major with important consequences (handling a case of suspected child neglect). Each decision may be handled in a somewhat different manner, and the same decision may be handled differently at different times. Nevertheless, certain decision-making patterns in a center tend to emerge based on the formal structure of the organization and the leadership style and beliefs of the director.

Decisions can be broadly classified as two types, those that are operational and relate to how staff carry out their respective jobs (for example, classroom or office activities), and those that are strategic and relate to the center as a whole (for example, program philosophy and center policies). But these global categories are inadequate in capturing the multidimensional nature of decision making in early childhood programs and identifying areas where the involvement of teachers, parents, and others may be increased. The following is a more comprehensive list of decision categories.

- staff supervision and professional development
- instructional practices and scheduling
- enrollment and grouping
- fiscal policies and practices
- human resource allocation
- centerwide goals and educational objectives
- parent relations
- community relations
- facilities management
- evaluation practices (child, staff, center)

The following table details 50 different decisions within these 10 categories. The list is by no means exhaustive, but it does give a representative sample of the many kinds of decisions that you and your staff make on a regular basis. Use this list as a template to begin thinking about the kinds of decisions that define the unique character of your program.

Types of Decisions in the Early Childhood Setting

1. **Staff supervision and professional development**

   - establish guidelines and procedures for staff orientation
   - establish guidelines for supervision of teaching staff
   - establish guidelines for supervision of support staff
   - determine the type and frequency of in-service training
   - establish career ladder guidelines

2. **Instructional practices and scheduling**

   - determine the daily schedule of classroom activities
   - select instructional materials and equipment
   - determine the content of the curriculum
   - determine the type and frequency of special events
   - establish an annual calendar

3. **Enrollment and grouping**

   - determine enrollment criteria and policies
   - determine group size and patterns (e.g., mixed-age grouping)
   - determine grouping assignments
   - determine adult-child ratios
   - determine the placement of children with special needs

4. **Fiscal policies and practices**

   - determine tuition and fees
   - determine salaries and benefits
   - set priorities for center and classroom expenditures
   - determine fundraising priorities and goals
   - determine the procedure for accounts payable and accounts receivable

5. **Human resource allocation**

   - determine the qualifications for different positions
   - determine staff hiring criteria and procedures
   - determine the staffing pattern and teaching assignments
   - set staff work schedules
   - determine the criteria for promotion and advancement

6. Centerwide goals and educational objectives

- determine the center's philosophy
- determine the educational objectives for different age groups
- determine the frequency and scheduling of staff meetings
- determine staff meeting agendas
- establish a code of conduct (e.g., dress, confidentiality)

7. Parent relations

- determine who serves as primary contact with parents
- set expectations for parent involvement
- determine the format and frequency of parent conferences
- determine the type and frequency of parent education
- determine the content of the parent newsletter

8. Community relations

- determine the type of contacts with community agencies
- establish marketing and public relations priorities
- determine the content of press releases
- establish a risk management plan
- determine the type of contact with local schools

9. Facilities management

- determine how space is allocated
- determine how space is arranged
- establish food service procedures and contracts
- determine capital improvement priorities
- determine maintenance procedures and contracts

10. Evaluation practices (child, staff, center)

- determine the type and frequency of child assessments
- determine guidelines for staff performance appraisals
- determine the type and frequency of programwide evaluations
- determine the center's accreditation timeline and procedures
- determine the use and distribution of evaluation data

What Are the Possible Levels of Participation?

The reason that participative management is such a complex concept to implement is that we cannot assume that greater participation is desirable in every situation—in other words, more is not always better. Determining the appropriate level of participation depends on the nature of the issue and the people involved. From the director's perspective, there are four levels of participation:

- unilateral
- consultative
- collaborative
- delegated

The following table delineates the subtle distinctions between levels:

Levels of Participation

1. **Unilateral decision making.** The director makes the decision.

    1.1 The director makes the decision and announces it to the staff.

    1.2 The director makes the decision and sells it to the staff, providing a rationale for a particular course of action.

2. **Consultative decision making.** Prior to making a decision, the director seeks information or ideas and suggestions from the staff.

    2.1 The director makes a tentative decision and solicits reactions from the staff (either individually or as a group) before making a final decision.

    2.2 The director presents the problem or issue to the staff and solicits suggestions and advice on solutions. The director then makes the decision, which may or may not reflect the staff's advice.

3. **Collaborative decision making.** The director and staff define and analyze problems together, generating and evaluating alternatives and deciding on a course of action.

    3.1 The final decision is made by unanimous vote.

    3.2 The final decision is made by majority vote.

    3.3 The final decision is made by consensus.

4. **Delegated decision making.** After providing relevant information, the director allows the staff to make the decision.

    4.1 The decision is made by a subgroup of the staff with or without input from others.

    4.2 The decision is made unilaterally by individual staff members.

Unilateral decision making is often referred to as the default decision-making style of center directors. It has strong appeal because it is quick, unencumbered, and more cost-effective in the short-term because it involves fewer people. The downside, of course, is that the staff may perceive unilateral decisions as arbitrary and authoritarian. From a decision-quality perspective, unilateral decision making can block good ideas that might ultimately be more cost effective.

Consultative decision making is an approach where board, teachers, parents, or children are asked to provide information, but the director reserves the right to make the final decision. This approach is attractive because it allows the director to sharpen and elaborate his or her position through discussion with others. *It is critical, however, that the director communicate up front how input from others will be used.* Failure to do so may leave group members uncertain as to the value of their contributions and may contribute to the possibility that a later announcement of the decision will be misunderstood.

Collaborative decision making generally takes more time, but if done properly, it can result in greater feelings of staff empowerment and commitment to the center. There are three ways that collaborative decisions can be achieved: a unanimous vote, a majority vote, or a consensus approach.

A decision made by unanimous vote means that everyone voting supports the decision. When lack of support or sabotage by one or more members could seriously damage an undertaking that requires total group support, a decision by unanimous vote may be necessary.

By avoiding conflicts arising from differences of opinion, the majority vote holds great attraction for many. But majority vote ascertains only those alternatives that people find more or less preferable (unless there is extended discussion). It does not uncover the alternatives that certain people find insupportable. One cannot assume that the loudest voices represent the feelings and opinions of quiet members. Some organizational theorists believe that a majority vote is not a rational group decision-making process because the discussion preceding it usually takes the form of persuasion, negotiation, and intimidation and may cut off discussion of viable alternatives.

In many organizations there exists a "strain toward convergence"—the desire to coalesce rapidly to avoid conflict-producing discussions. Particularly in hierarchically differentiated groups, lower-level participants tend to remain silent about their ideas or acquiesce to what they perceive to be the majority opinion. Often individuals may feel, I don't actually agree with that idea, but no one else seems to be saying anything, so I won't rock the boat. Being aware of the desire to avoid conflict and the need to compromise is particularly important when dealing with predominantly female groups. Women in general tend to take the role of harmonizer or compromiser.

Consensus strategies seek to generate general agreement on an issue. For consensus to exist, it is not necessary for every participant to agree in full, but it is necessary for every person to be heard and, in the end, for none to believe that the decision violates his or her convictions. The decision may not represent everyone's first choice, but those who remain doubtful nevertheless understand the decision and agree not to obstruct its implementation.

Consensus means. . .

- all team members are able to paraphrase the issue to show they understand it

- all team members have a chance to voice their opinions on the issue

- all team members share the final decision

- all team members agree to take responsibility for implementing the decision

Consensus does not mean . . .

- a decision by unanimous vote

- the final decision is everyone's first choice

- there are no differences of opinion

Because consensus-building strategies take more time and often require advanced skill in communication and conflict resolution, decision by consensus is more difficult to achieve than is decision by a majority vote. Chapter 8 includes several different consensus-building strategies you may want to try at your center. The emotional boost to staff that results makes these strategies worth implementing when possible, particularly when considering complex issues or making decisions that have centerwide implications.

Delegated decision making essentially turns over the responsibility for making the decision to another individual or group. When an individual or a group is given unilateral authority for making a decision, caution needs to be taken that the arrangement is not perceived as favoritism, creating a sense of competition or resentment among other stakeholders. Success rests on the appropriate match of people and activities. It is also essential that the scope of the decision and the methods of accountability are clear.

The diagram below depicts directors' and teachers' zone of control and influence as they relate to the four decision-making approaches.

**Zones of Control as They Relate to the
Four Decision-Making Approaches**

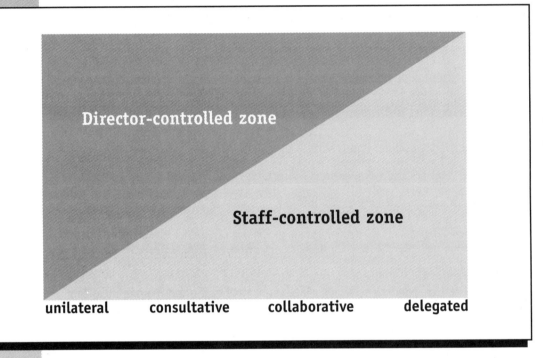

Now that you have an understanding of the different levels of participation in decision making, look back at your answers to Exercise 4 on page 16. Use the following table to code your responses to this exercise. Your results will give you an idea of your current decision-making style.

Preferred Decision-Making Styles

Statement			Style
1	8	10	Unilateral
3	9	12	Consultative
2	4	7	Collaborative
5	6	11	Delegated

What Are the External Constraints?

Consultative, collaborative, and delegated decision-making approaches have strong appeal from a participative management perspective because they involve individuals in the process who might otherwise be excluded. Such involvement can result in feelings of empowerment. Despite directors' good intentions to expand the decision-making influence of different stakeholders in their programs, however, the realities of the job often prevent directors from carrying through. Four external constraints are:

- time
- resources
- mandates
- staff stability

Speed is clearly not an advantage of shared decision making. When faced with an impending epidemic of head lice, for example, directors simply do not have the luxury of involving others before taking action. The circumstances of certain kinds of decisions dictate swift unilateral action.

The lack of financial resources needed to pay staff to attend staff meetings or to provide incentives for greater involvement, as well, often limits a director's ability to involve others broadly in centerwide decision making. In addition, there are certain mandates from sponsoring agencies, boards, and other regulating bodies that can limit a director's options.

Finally, lack of program stability caused by high staff turnover can severely hamper a director's engaging in a more participative approach. Shared decision making is most successful when staff are informed, understand centerwide issues, and have made a long-term commitment to the organization.

Obstacles notwithstanding, there is much that can be done to foster greater involvement in decision making in early childhood programs. The next chapter helps you begin that process.

CHAPTER 5

The Decision-Making Process

Under what conditions should involvement in decision making be expanded? The answer to that question varies from situation to situation, given the needs of the people involved, the time frame in which to make the decision and involve people, and the levels of expertise they have.

Who Should Be Involved in Making Decisions?

In determining how to involve stakeholders in the decision-making process, you need to determine the decisions in which individuals have a high interest and the expertise to contribute helpfully. Two tests will help guide these deliberations:

- **Test of relevance.** Do the individuals have a personal stake in the decision? If they have a strong personal stake, their interest in participating will be high. If they have no personal stake, they will be content to defer to someone else.

- **Test of expertise.** To what extent are the stakeholders competent and qualified to make a useful contribution to the identification or solution of the problem? Do they have the knowledge and skill to be able to make an informed and wise decision?

The decision-making model derived from these two tests is quite straightforward. It merely describes four situations in which the degree of involvement decreases depending on the combination of interest and expertise of the stakeholders.

- **Situation 1 – Low interest, low expertise.** If the topic or issue is irrelevant and falls outside the sphere of competence of the stakeholders, then involvement should be avoided. Indeed, involvement in this case is likely to produce resentment because subordinates typically will not want to be involved and will probably not follow through if delegated tasks.

- **Situation 2 – Low interest, high expertise.** In this situation, it is usually best to limit the involvement of other stakeholders to a consultative model of decision making. To involve others at a deeper level may increase the likelihood of alienation. Although the involvement of others under these circumstances increases the director's chances of reaching a higher-quality decision, the disinterested parties are likely to wonder, What does the director get paid for anyway?

- **Situation 3 – High interest, low expertise.** This situation needs careful consideration and skillful leadership. Involvement of various stakeholders should be limited. The rationale for involvement here is to lower resistance to the decision. A consultative model of participation may be useful in this situation so that the interested parties have input, but the director makes the final decision.

- **Situation 4 – High interest, high expertise.** If people have a personal stake (high relevance) in the decision and have the knowledge to make a useful contribution (high expertise), they should be involved in the decision-making process as early as possible and given as much freedom as possible in defining the problem and specifying objectives either as a delegated approach or as a collaborative approach.

Four Situations Indicating the Degree of Stakeholders' Interest and Expertise

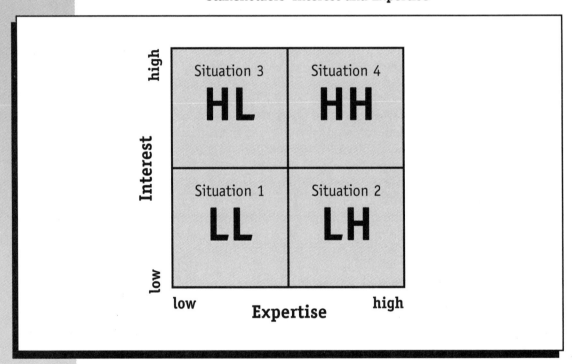

Making Good Decisions

Making good decisions does not happen by accident. It involves a systematic process of identifying the problem or issue, collecting data, weighing alternatives, and deciding on a course of action.

Ten Steps for Making Successful Decisions

1. Identify and explicitly state the issue that needs to be resolved or the problem that needs to be solved.

2. Identify the key stakeholders whose interests need to be considered in the decision-making process.

3. Assess how strongly each stakeholder feels about the issue—his or her level of interest— as well as his or her level of expertise regarding the issue.

4. Determine the appropriate level of participation of different stakeholders.

5. Identify any constraints that may affect the scope or content of the decision (e.g., time, budget, human resources, external mandates).

6. State explicitly any important values that should be maintained in reaching the final decision. (For example, "Whatever proposal comes forward, we want to maintain small group sizes and maximize teacher-child contact.")

7. Make clear the timeline for deciding and implementing the decision.

8. Make the decision or recommendation.

9. Communicate the reasons for the decision, including how people's input was used, fully and clearly to all interested parties.

10. Evaluate the decision-making process and the outcome of the decision.

The diamond diagram below illustrates the three phases of communication needed to move a group to a decision based on consensus. During the creativity stage, ideas are generated using open-ended questions, effective listening strategies, brainstorming techniques, and recording of ideas on a flip chart. The goal at this stage is to open up the discussion to a wide range of creative possibilities. Once all ideas have been shared, moving into the second phase of analysis is easier. This is where the group clarifies items, notes patterns, combines and groups suggestions, and evaluates the merits of each contribution. The challenge during this second phase is to keep the group focused. Finally, during the decision phase the group summarizes, eliminates, and narrows the field of possibilities through rank ordering, prioritizing, or voting.

I t is by
logic that
we prove. It is
by intuition that
we discover.

Henri Poincare

**Decision Diamond Depicting Three Phases
of Making a Decision by Consensus**

Creativity
Open discussion to
generate and record ideas

Analysis
Clarify and group items,
chart patterns, evaluate impact,
and assess outcomes

Decision
Eliminate and narrow, prioritize,
rank, or vote to determine
most suitable alternative

*Adapted from Pokras, S. (1997). Working in teams (p. 75). Menlo Park, CA: Crisp Publications.
Reprinted with permission.*

Assessing the Impact of Decisions

Another way to think about decision making is through the model of input-output analysis: What are the costs of a particular course of action in terms of money, time, and human resources as compared to its short- and long-term effects? Impact, as well, can be thought of in economic terms (e.g., more income generated for the center), in political or social terms (e.g., a competitive edge over other centers), or in human terms (e.g., increased employee motivation, commitment, and job satisfaction).

There are several questions to keep in mind when anticipating the potential impact of different courses of action.

- **How far into the future does the decision commit the center?** If a decision can be reversed easily, it should probably be made quickly. On the other hand, if the impact of the decision will have long-term consequences for the center, then careful consideration and a systematic assessment of different alternatives deserves your time.

- **What areas of the center will be affected by the decision?** If the decision will impact only one area of the organization (the infant classrooms, for example), the decision should be made at that level.

- **What values, ethical principles, strongly-held beliefs, or philosophical tenets enter into the decision?** If a decision impacts core values and beliefs of any of the center staff in any way, then an effort should be made to involve those parties in making the decision.

- **What is the likelihood that the decision will need to be made again?** If the issue being decided is unique, then the decision-making process should be treated as a distinct event. On the other hand, if the issue is is likely to recur, then establishing a rule or guidelines for making the decision is important so that in the future such decisions can be made swiftly.

One might say that there are only two types of decisions: those that are expensive to change and those that are not. A decision to expand the program to include infant care should not be made hastily, nor without plenty of input from staff, parents, and other interested parties. But common decisions, like what kind of easel paint to purchase, should be made quickly. These decisions, if wrong, can be corrected inexpensively later.

Striving for Flexibility and Balance

Sometimes people get bogged down in the decision-making process because they try too hard to be objective. Not only is complete objectivity impossible, it may even be counterproductive. People by their very nature are a quirky mixture of rational and emotional components. Accept the fact that your emotions and the emotions of your staff will enter into the decision-making process. Sound decision making is a balance between relying on facts (a logical analysis of the data) and intuition (that powerful feeling in your gut that tells you how to proceed).

The person who insists upon seeing with perfect clarity before he decides, never decides.

Henri Frederic Amiel

Others get bogged down in the decision-making process because they are never quite sure they have enough data or have carefully analyzed all alternatives to make an informed decision. Just how much data or analysis is enough varies from situation to situation, depending on the importance of the decision (its potential impact) and the time constraints on making the decision.

How people approach the decision-making process is related largely to their psychological preferences. Some people have a strong need for closure and they make quick decisions and move on. Other people are very cautious in making decisions, preferring to keep possibilities open and explore all alternatives thoroughly before committing themselves to a course of action.

Finding the right balance between these two styles is the essence of effective leadership. Good decision making means gathering sufficient information (facts, figures, people's opinions) and spending sufficient time analyzing alternatives. Spending too much time making a decision can lead to a "paralysis of analysis" and negatively impact an organization's ability to respond to change.

> *The other day I had the opportunity to meet the company President. While I was in his office I asked him, "Sir, What is the secret of your success?"*
>
> *He said, "Two words."*
>
> *"And, Sir, what are they?"*
>
> *"Right decisions."*
>
> *"But how do you make right decisions?"*
>
> *"One word," he responded.*
>
> *"And, sir, what is that?"*
>
> *"Experience."*
>
> *"And how do you get experience?"*
>
> *"Two words," he responded.*
>
> *"And, Sir, what are they?"*
>
> *"Wrong decisions."*

Now let's put your new knowledge about shared decision making to work by completing Exercise 6. The next chapter includes additional suggestions for formalizing the process.

Think of a decision to be made within the next month that has centerwide implications. It need not be a major decision, simply one that provides an opportunity to expand the circle of influence of some of the people with whom you work.

Describe the issue or problem: _____

_____

Who are the stakeholders who may be affected by the decision?

Stakeholder	Relevance			Expertise		
_____	L	M	H	L	M	H
_____	L	M	H	L	M	H
_____	L	M	H	L	M	H
_____	L	M	H	L	M	H
_____	L	M	H	L	M	H

For each stakeholder, assess the level of interest in the issue (low, medium, or high relevance) and the level of competence to make an informed and wise decision (low, medium, or high expertise).

Referring to the table on page 23, what level of participation do you think would be most effective to use in this situation: consultative, collaborative, or delegated?

_____

What are the external constraints that may impact stakeholders' involvement?

_____

Describe your strategy: _____

_____

_____

_____

CHAPTER 6

Participative Management: Getting Started

It all begins with the director. You are the key person to initiate and facilitate a model of participative management and shared decision making at your center. If it is going to happen, it will do so because of your commitment to the process. You are the one who must provide the necessary support—time, resources, and encouragement—to sustain teachers' collegial interaction. It is not enough to embrace the beliefs and values surrounding participation. Organizational structures and processes must be adapted so that staff and other stakeholders have the power and capacity to participate actively in decision-making ventures.

Changing decision-making structures and processes must be approached carefully. You don't want to abandon current structures before examining them to determine exactly what should be improved. Your goal should be to improve the process of decision making no matter what formal structures are created to support it. When decisions are viewed as legitimate, people feel invested and can therefore accept decisions, even those that are contrary to their personal views.

How Interested Are Your Teachers in Making Decisions?

The first step in implementing a model of shared decision making is to work with staff, board, and parents to define the types of decisions that need to be made, current levels of participation, and desired levels of involvement. You cannot assume, for example, that all teachers have the same desire for greater participation in centerwide decisions.

Teachers are not homogeneous in attitudes, sentiments, and expectations concerning decision making. Different people want different things, depending on what is going on in their personal lives and on their long-range career goals. Indeed, teachers resent being involved in trivial matters, serving on committees of dubious value, and sitting through long meetings on topics that are of little interest to them.

The Decision-Making Influence Questionnaire found in Appendix A can help you assess teachers' participation in decision making in relative terms (how much influence they currently have compared to how much they want). Understanding the discrepancy between current and desired levels of decision-making influence will help you know how to structure your efforts. The questionnaire also includes questions about how staff perceive the decision-making process at your center.

Make copies of the Decision-Making Influence Questionnaire and distribute it to teachers who work at your center more than ten hours per week. Give each person a blank envelope in which to put the completed questionnaire. Place a box labeled Questionnaire Return Box in your center's office or staff room, and ask staff to put their completed questionnaires in. The scoring key for the questionnaire can be found in Appendix B.

It is important to let your staff know who will be summarizing the data (you, a secretary, a board member). Also let them know how you intend to use the information collected from the survey. If you intend to summarize the data and share the results at a staff meeting, be sure to indicate this in your cover memo. Your invitation to staff to share their perceptions about current and desired decision-making influence can serve as a springboard for a group discussion about how to expand decision-making influence at the center.

Compare the scores from the Decision-Making Influence Questionnaire with the scores you estimated when you completed Exercise 3 on page 3. How accurate were your estimates of your staff's current and desired levels of decision-making influence? How large is the discrepancy between their current and desired levels of decision-making influence?

The Importance of Trust—And How to Build It

In early childhood centers, as in all organizations, things tend to get done because of relationships, not because of job descriptions or formal roles. Research suggests that teachers' willingness to participate in decision making is influenced primarily by their relationships with their director. Merely establishing policies and procedures for staff participation in decision making will not necessarily result in greater participation; interpersonal trust is essential if shared decision making is to take hold. Trust begins with one-on-one connections—getting to know staff individually. Conversely, problems between directors and staff or among colleagues are often the result of distrust. Distrust begins when each party assumes that the other operates from self-interest with little regard for the interests of others.

Elements of a Supportive Environment

To create a supportive environment . . .

✓ avoid pressuring people to participate

✓ encourage divergent points of view

✓ presume people's intentions to be positive

✓ avoid "one-right-answer" thinking

✓ encourage risk taking

Directors who have successfully broadened participation emphasize that it is important to avoid pressuring individuals to participate; coercion causes resentment. It is also important to avoid a bandwagon mentality because everyone may jump on, but some will jump off when the spotlights are dimmed. If you offer incentives, they should not be so attractive that everyone will volunteer, whether or not they intend to follow through on their commitments. For the same reason, directors should not impose sanctions on those who refuse to participate.

An open and trusting environment is nurtured when divergent points of view are encouraged. People must be allowed to register their feelings without fear of censure. When groups are too cohesive or too like-minded, they can promote blind uniformity. The problem with uniformity is that it can produce an uncritical acceptance of an idea. This may result in a phenomenon known as groupthink.

Your ability to encourage divergent points of view rests on your ability to appreciate the diversity in people's value structures. Value orientations are determined by cultural traditions, experience, and deeply held beliefs. The only way you can communicate that you truly value differing perspectives is by employing empathetic listening skills and acting in ways that validates others' views.

An open, trusting environment is cultivated when directors avoid one-right-answer thinking. Most problems can be solved in a number of good ways. Keeping options open and exploring new, creative ways to define and solve problems communicates to staff that different perceptions of the issue are both valued and valuable in generating ideas for collective action.

One of the paradoxes of organizational life is that even when teachers express a desire for more decision-making influence than they currently have, many teachers will shy away from the invitation to become more involved. Sometimes people fail to get involved because they don't believe that their actions will lead to changes. Other times resistance can be explained by fear of failure or fear of making a mistake. The risk of taking on something new brings with it the possibility that those involved will not be viewed as competent. Some people, by nature, are just more averse to risk—they prefer to complain about injustices than become vulnerable by getting involved and making changes.

Be sensitive to your teachers' ambivalence about getting involved in centerwide decision making. Your role is crucial in establishing a positive, open atmosphere that actively supports teachers' growth—one that encourages risktaking and recognizes the lessons to be learned from mistakes.

In organizations where everyone thinks alike, no one thinks very much.

Walter Lippmann

You need to create an environment in which no one is afraid to tell the emperor that he has no clothes.

Bill Fromm

Bringing People Together

The process of evaluating and modifying current decision-making processes to achieve a more participative style of management will take many months. One way to initiate the process is to schedule a staff retreat—a full day, in a setting away from your center, where you, your board, your staff, and other key stakeholders can focus on the work at hand.

Several weeks prior to the retreat, have participants complete the Decision-Making Influence Questionnaire. The summary data generated from this instrument can serve as a springboard for your discussion. Have copies of Different Types of Decisions on hand (see pp. 21-22). You may want to add more items under each category so that the final list accurately reflects the unique character of your center. Also have on hand copies of Levels of Participation (see p.23).

Your goal for the day should be to have everyone examine the full range of decisions made at your center, the consequences of those decisions, and how the current decision-making process affects people. Most likely, you will discover that the types of decision making fall into three broad categories:

- unilateral decisions that are best made by the center's owner, board of directors, or by you the director because of the legal requirements of the center or the need for confidentiality of information;

- decisions that can be made with the combined input of staff and administration either through a consultative or collaborative approach; and

- delegated decisions that can be made by the teachers or support staff exclusively.

In applying this framework, you may find that the lines between teachers' responsibilities and those of administrators become blurred. This happens because many decisions in early childhood settings span educational and administrative domains.

For decisions in the consultative category, it is important at the outset to determine who will be involved and how their input will be used. When employees are under the false impression that their input will influence the final decision, a willingness to commit to implementing the decision may be jeopardized if their suggestions are not used. Thus it is essential that you be forthright about how you intend to use the information you solicit in your consultative approach.

For decisions in the collaborative and delegated categories, you must determine the different roles of stakeholders, the resources available, the timelines that will guide the decision-making process, and the degree of each participant's accountability. This may take several months to accomplish.

If, in the past, you have had a predominantly unilateral decision-making model at your center, take small steps to broaden participation until you and your staff feel comfortable with the staff's expanded influence. For example, the arrangement of space and materials in the classroom, work schedules, and assignment of rotating responsibilities can be made collaboratively with teachers at first and then turned over to them entirely when you feel they have the interest and expertise to make those decisions. In the consultative area, begin to involve teachers in the screening and interviewing of new staff and invite their input on centerwide policies that affect them. Over time, these small steps will do much to increase feelings of involvement and improve overall morale.

Changing Structures and Processes

Winston Churchill said, "We shape our buildings, and afterwards our buildings shape us." The same might be said about the structures and processes of the organizations in which we work.

The structures and processes of an organization must be consistent with the management philosophy that guides it. Many centers' structures inhibit teachers from participating fully in decision making. Moving toward more collaborative structures usually means moving away from hierarchical pyramid structures and centralized communication processes toward a representational form where power and decision making are more evenly distributed (e.g., interlocking circles, web of connecting pods) and communication more widely dispersed.

Not all hierarchical structures are inherently bad. Large hierarchically structured programs can use a participative approach while, conversely, flat organizational structures such as parent cooperatives can be dominated and controlled by one person. More important than formal structure are the kinds of organizational processes that define how work is carried out.

In finding ways to expand the circle of influence of the stakeholders at your center, you may need to develop new organizational structures—a management team, an advisory committee, or an ad hoc group that focuses on a special area of decision making. New structures and processes for staff meetings are particularly important to ensure input from teachers and to rotate the task of facilitating meetings.

Other new structures may include quality circles or advisory teams. Quality circles are small groups of teachers who meet regularly to identify, document, and recommend solutions within their work area. The rationale behind quality circles is that the people performing a job are the best people to diagnose problems in their work and to recommend solutions. Quality circles are effective in uniting teachers around center improvement efforts. Some directors use the quality circle concept to organize teams during the self-study process of NAEYC accreditation.

A center's communication structure and processes can also have a strong impact on employee's participation. Think for a moment about who controls the flow of written communication in your center. Who has the authority to post information? Who determines what is stated about the center in written pieces—brochures or the parent handbook? Opening communication processes to wider participation does not have to result in disagreement and chaos. Coordination of information is essential in an organization, but there may be ways to encourage broader input into what information is disseminated and how.

The center's physical environment, staff schedules, and structure of role relationships have an impact on your ability to implement a model of participative management. Teachers need adequate space (with adult-size furniture) and work schedules that encourage and support collaborative meetings to plan and work together on different tasks.

Structures and Processes That Support Participative Management

Structures that support participative management . . .

- de-emphasize the chain of command and hierarchical differentiation
- provide staff with opportunities to exercise initiative

Processes that support participative management . . .

- provide training and experience to help staff express their ideas persuasively and operate effectively in groups
- encourage a free-flowing expression of information and ideas
- de-emphasize conflict avoidance through forcing, smoothing, or ignoring
- encourage high levels of participation and influence regardless of status position

Adapted from Wood, C. J. (1984). Participatory decision making: Why doesn't it seem to work? Educational Forum, 49 (1), 59.

Group Size

One problem of shared decision making is that the size of the group can affect the quality of a decision and the dynamics of the group process. As the number of participants increases in any decision-making process, coordination becomes more important and more difficult. Some things to keep in mind:

- A group of five to nine members usually performs better than an individual tackling the same task. This group size seems to provide the best mix of resources and encourage comfortable give and take.

- A group with fewer than five members often fails to outperform an individual either because too few perspectives are represented or the group is too easily dominated by one member.

- A group with more than nine members often fails to outperform individuals because it is too large for everyone to participate and make a valuable contribution.

- Groups with an even number of members may divide into two subgroups over volatile issues.

Putting It in Writing

There are several advantages to putting your center's decision-making guidelines in writing. Writing out a plan helps clarify thinking and the finished document serves as a mechanism for ongoing evaluation of the decision-making structure of the center. This process is also a way to introduce new staff to the concept of shared decision making.

Appendix C presents a decision-making blueprint for a large child development center. This list of key decision-making processes was compiled over 14 months by the director and her staff, and you may find it useful in implementing new decision-making processes at your center.

CHAPTER 7

Case Studies – Collaboration in Action

Should a center expand its services to include infants? Should the program merge with another agency? Should the center require CDAs for all assistant teachers? Should the program include more academics in the curriculum, as requested by parents? These are some of the many difficult issues that directors face in administering their programs.

The following case studies offer a glimpse into the decision-making styles of four directors confronted with making important decisions about their programs. See you if agree with the approach each took.

Patricia Makes a Unilateral Decision

Patricia is the director of a large nonprofit child care program. In her fourth year of administering the center, she was confronted with a situation requiring the termination of an employee.

John, the maintenance man, was well liked, knew the job, took pride in the center, and took the time to build a rapport with the children, staff, and parents. However, John was a recovering alcoholic, and at times he had difficulty coping with daily stress. Twice he did not show up for work for three consecutive days and did not call in or give an explanation for his absence.

The first time this happened, Patricia gave John a strong verbal warning with the understanding that he would regularly attend Alcoholics Anonymous meetings and get counseling to learn how to handle stress. He was told that future incidents would result in further discipline that could include termination.

The second setback occurred only three months later. Again John was gone for three days. This time Patricia gave him a written warning and stated that another incident would result in his termination.

On the third occasion, Patricia terminated John. She sent the following memo to her staff: "John turned in his keys today and will no longer be working at our center. I regret this necessary action. Until a replacement is found, please try to handle all minor maintenance issues yourself, and refer all major requests to me." Patricia felt comfortable making a unilateral decision to terminate John, but she was unprepared for its repercussions.

The memo caused an uproar; the teachers were angry and wanted an explanation. Several stormed into Patricia's office to express their discontent. John's history had never been discussed with the staff, nor were the reasons why he was, at times, gone for several days. To the staff, Patricia's decision seemed arbitrary and unfair. Patricia realized that the situation could get quickly out of hand if the teachers started talking to parents. She did not want any rumors spread. She decided to convene a staff meeting to explain her actions.

At the meeting, Patricia expressed her appreciation for the staff's support of a co-worker. She pointed out that for reasons of confidentiality she was not at liberty to discuss the events leading up to John's termination. She acknowledged John's good work and the strong relationships he had cultivated with the staff and children.

Then Patricia made the following statement: "I trust you to make wise decisions in your classrooms. I cannot participate in every decision that you make that affects the children in your care. I know you are thoughtful, caring people who would not make a decision that would purposely hurt or demean another person. I hope you will extend the same trust and understanding to me. I had a difficult decision to make, and I made it for the good of the program. Just as you would not want me to discuss your history with anyone else, I ask that you respect John's privacy in the same way."

When Patricia finished, there was an awkward moment of silence. Then one teacher broke the tension by apologizing for her emotional response the previous day. Another said, "But what do we do until we hire a replacement for John? We're all working so hard. It doesn't seem fair that we now have maintenance responsibilities too."

Patricia seized the opportunity for collaborative decision making. The teachers agreed to assume responsibilities for their own classrooms and bathrooms if given the necessary equipment and supplies. They drafted a list of essentials. Patricia listened as they channeled their anger into positive and productive solutions to the immediate crisis.

It was several weeks before a new maintenance person was hired. To announce the hiring decision, Patricia issued another memo thanking her staff for their patience and hard work in the interim. She also asked them to come to the next staff meeting with some creative ideas for spending the $600 in personnel costs that had been saved since John's departure.

In reflecting on this incident, Patricia still feels that the termination decision was one that she alone could make. She says, however, that she probably should have announced her decision at a staff meeting rather than through a formal memo. She had not realized the deep personal attachment that teachers and support staff had developed with John and how his departure might bring to the surface their own insecurities about their jobs. Announcing her decision in person might have softened the shock and loss they experienced. It also would have given Patricia an opportunity to acknowledge how hard her staff was working and elicit their support during the transition.

Mark and Sylvia's Consultative Decision Making

Mark and Sylvia own and operate a private for-profit child care center. Like most administrators who own and direct their own centers, they make numerous facility management decisions every month relating to landscaping, heating and ventilation, plumbing, and playground maintenance. One fairly routine decision they had made unilaterally in the past was about replacing playground surfacing material. In their center's 20 years of operation, they had tried everything—woodchips, sand, crushed pebbles, and recycled rubber. They have also heard all the laments from parents and teachers about the pros and cons of different surfaces —sand gets tracked into the building, woodchips get caught in the lawnmower, pebbles get thrown at other children, children scrape their knees landing on the rubber groundcover.

In an attempt to expand the decision-making influence of different stakeholders at their center, Mark and Sylvia decided to ask volunteers to serve as playground consultants to them and make a recommendation about what type of new surfacing they should purchase for the playground. They made it clear that they were looking for advice and recommendations; they would retain the final decision-making authority in this situation.

Mark and Sylvia put the word out in the parent newsletter and posted their request on the staff bulletin board. Much to their surprise, three parents and four teachers were eager to be part of the consultant team. The three parents asked if their children could be included since they were also very interested in the outcome of the decision. The janitor (who also doubled as landscape gardener) also asked to be part of the team.

Mark and Sylvia designated a teacher volunteer to serve as the official captain of the playground consultant team. The group selected eight playgrounds in the community to visit. It took two Saturdays to visit all the sites and to talk to vendors about the advantages and costs of different options. The team then assembled a three-page handwritten evaluation of the different surfacing options they had submitted to Mark and Sylvia. The evaluation even included photographs and the children's comments about what it was like to jump off a playground structure onto different surfaces.

Mark and Sylvia treated the group to dinner at a restaurant where they gave the team a rousing thank you for its hard work. They also posted the results of the team's efforts on the parent bulletin board and included a note of thanks in the center's newsletter.

In reflecting on this situation, Mark admitted that he was downright surprised that parents and teachers would volunteer to give up two Saturdays without any monetary remuneration. He was taken back when they told him they felt honored to be asked to serve on this team. Sylvia was surprised by the level of enthusiasm the experience generated—the parents and teachers genuinely had fun on their Saturday playground excursions. The situation has led Mark and Sylvia to consider additional areas of decision making in which their staff might have some influence.

Theresa and Her Staff – Decision Making by Consensus

Theresa directs a small full-day program for 30 children. In early June she was approached by a parent who wanted to enroll her child for just seven weeks.

At most centers such a decision would be merely a matter of determining whether the enrollment jeopardized the licensed capacity of the center. At Theresa's center, however, the decision had more important philosophical and operational consequences. Her program is founded on the belief that developing a secure attachment between a child and the teacher is the key to quality child care. Enrolling a child for just seven weeks would disrupt normal classroom procedures and create a challenging situation for the teacher and other children.

From an administrative standpoint, there was a compelling case for admitting the student. If the center operated without full enrollment, Theresa and her board would need to increase their fundraising efforts to maintain a balanced budget. But Theresa realized that her staff were also strong stakeholders with a high interest in the outcome. They would have to adjust their teaching practices to accommodate the new child in the group for a limited time. Their focus on developing a secure attachment would have to be modified.

Theresa had worked hard to develop a sense of professional autonomy at her center. Making a decision without involving her staff would send the wrong signal. Theresa convened a meeting with her teachers. For two hours they analyzed the problem, weighed the alternatives, and decided on a plan of action. Their final decision, made by consensus, was to enroll the child.

In reflecting on this situation, Theresa admits that it would have been simpler to have made a unilateral decision to enroll the child. But the time invested in the collaborative decision-making process was well spent. She is sure that the outcomes for the child and parent would not have been as positive if the entire staff had not "bought in to" the decision.

Shared decision making on this issue had a greater benefit. The center is facing the challenges of meeting the community's changing demographics. Theresa knows that her center will need to make major adjustments in the future if her program is to survive. The process of collaboration on this relatively small issue had an ancillary benefit. She believes she now has a model in place for making changes that touch the sensitive nerve of her center's philosophy of care and education without destroying it.

Michelle Delegates a Decision

Michelle is the director of a Head Start program sponsored by a large social services agency. For years her center has held a formal graduation ceremony when the children complete Head Start and move on to kindergarten. Last year, however, the agency asked Michelle to stop holding the graduation ceremony. The rationale was that the ceremony placed too much stress on the children and parents and that it was too expensive for the agency.

Michelle had mixed feelings about abandoning the ceremony. In the years when she worked at an affluent suburban program, such a practice would have been viewed as inappropriate, if not downright silly. But in the cultural context of the Head Start program, it was neither silly nor inappropriate. Far from causing stress for the children and parents, she recognized that graduation was a moment of immense pride for the community. Children and parents eagerly anticipated the ceremony. The children recited songs and poems; relatives and community representatives attended. Afterward, photographs always appeared in the local newspaper.

When Michelle shared the agency's decision with her parent board, they were very upset. Within a week of her meeting, she received numerous calls from parents expressing concern about the change. Some parents shared with her the belief that in their family, graduation from Head Start might be their children's only graduation. Michelle was moved by the emotional weight of their appeal.

Michelle called her supervisor at the agency's central office and explained her dilemma. How could she implement a decision that would cause such disappointment among the parents? Her supervisor advised her to handle the situation in a way that respected the needs of the community but did not cost the agency any money.

Michelle first met with her teachers to see how they felt about the issue. All agreed that hosting the graduation ceremony involved an enormous investment of time on their part, but they felt it was worthwhile because it helped them achieve their educational and parent relations goals.

Michelle convened a special meeting of the parent board. She invited the teachers and all parents to attend. She was surprised that more parents showed up for this meeting than for the parent orientation she had hosted the previous month. She indicated that she would delegate to the parent board the final decision of whether to hold graduation. However, if the board decided affirmatively, they would need to decide how the event would be financed.

For three hours the group debated different issues: Was it really necessary for the children to wear caps and gowns? Yes. Would parents be willing to pay for the cost of renting caps and gowns? No. Could enough money be raised from local merchants to cover the cost of renting space? Not sure. Would parents be willing to make and serve food? Yes. Would a photographer be willing to donate services for the event? Not sure.

The group adjourned without coming to a final decision, but agreed to reconvene in one month after some phone calls and personal visits had been made to local merchants. When the second meeting was held, the board decided that there was strong enough commitment to proceed with the celebration, but that the scale would be determined by the financial resources available. A formal parent/teacher committee was formed. Six months later, a very joyful graduation celebration took place, complete with caps and gowns and professional photographs.

In reflecting on this experience, Michelle says she learned a valuable lesson about the importance of delegating decisions when the stakeholders feel strongly about an issue and have the competence and expertise to carry it out. Both Michelle and her teachers were pleasantly surprised at the positive spin-off of increased parent commitment to the program. They are grateful that their agency was amenable to working out a win/win solution to this issue.

These four case studies demonstrate that there are a number of ways to increase shared decision making in early childhood programs. All the approaches require time and commitment to the process, but each can result in wonderful unanticipated benefits to both the program and the individuals involved.

CHAPTER 8

Strategies That Encourage Participation

To open up and expand the decision-making influence of your staff, you may need to modify your leadership style. Learning a variety of group facilitation skills—effective questioning, active listening, soliciting feedback, balancing discussion and dialogue, brainstorming, recording ideas, and building consensus—will help you achieve your goal.

Beyond group facilitation skills, it is also important that essential roles be played in group meetings (facilitating, clarifying, summarizing) and that meeting tasks be performed (agendas distributed, minutes accurately recorded) so that your staff can function effectively.

This chapter summarizes some effective strategies for encouraging participation. A more complete treatment of group dynamics in meetings is provided in *Making the Most of Meetings*, another book in the Directors' Toolbox Management Series.

Asking the Right Questions

Inviting staff to express their views and opinions, clarifying understanding, and requesting contributions from all involved are ways the director can encourage participation and foster greater involvement. Effective questioning is another way to promote participation.

Effective questioning is achieved only through practice and self-evaluation after each situation. The following table presents some questions that can be used in groups to broaden and focus discussion as well as to move the group along toward a decision.

Questions designed to open up discussion

1. What do you think about the problem as stated?

2. What has your experience been in dealing with this problem?

3. Would anyone care to offer suggestions for gathering facts to improve our understanding of the problem?

Questions designed to broaden participation

1. Now that we have heard from a number of you, would others who have not spoken like to add their ideas?

2. How do the ideas presented so far sound to those of you who have not yet shared your reactions?

3. What other aspects of the problem should be explored?

Questions designed to focus discussion

1. Where are we now in relation to our goal for this discussion?

2. Would you like to have me review the things we have said and the progress we have made in this discussion?

3. Your comment is interesting, but I wonder if it is relevant to the problem that is before us.

Questions designed to help the group reach a decision

1. Am I right in sensing agreement on these points? (Leader then gives a brief summary.)

2. Since we seem to be moving in the direction of a decision, should we consider what it will mean for our group if we decide the matter this way?

3. What have we accomplished in our discussion up to this point?

Adapted from Glickman, C. D. (1985). <u>Supervision of instruction.</u> Boston: Allyn & Bacon.

Accomplished facilitators never embarrass or surprise group members. They know how to introduce and pace questions to ensure active participation. Below are some guidelines for asking nonthreatening questions.

Asking Nonthreatening Questions

- Begin by asking a question of your entire team rather than singling out an individual and putting that person on the spot.

    Example: "What are the possible reasons why the children are having problems with transitions at lunch?" (Do not say, "Jane, what are the possible reasons the children are having problems with transitions?")

- Don't be afraid of silence. Some directors become anxious if a question does not elicit an immediate response. If this happens to you, relax; your teachers are thinking.

- If a teacher responds, acknowledge the remark and explore the response further if possible. For example,

    Teacher: "One of the reasons we are having problems with transitions at lunch is that the new cook brings in the food cart and just leaves it by the door."

    Director: "Why is leaving the food cart by the door contributing to the transition problem at lunch?"

    Teacher: "Well, before, the cook put the food on the table while we got the kids washed and ready. Now, one of us has to get the food on the table, leaving only one person to do the handwashing."

- If no one responds in a reasonable amount of time, look for nonverbal signals from a staff member who is wanting to be involved (i.e., eye contact, a forward lean, an uplifted eyebrow.) Then, call on that person by name.

    Example: "Letitia, you look as if you have something to offer here. Can you help us out? In your opinion, what are the possible reasons the children are having transition problems at lunch?"

- If no one responds to a question, consider rewording the question or asking if the question needs clarification.

    Example: "Have I explained this clearly?" (rather than, "Do you understand?")

- Ask questions that are not biased.

  Example: "What may be causing the problem?" (Do not say, "Is the problem caused by rushing the children? The problem may be caused by more than one factor.)

- Avoid too many yes/no questions. These have the effect of limiting discussion.

  Example: "Is the transition problem caused by understaffing?" (You will probably get "yes" or "no" answers, but little discussion.)

- Pose questions that do not put your teachers on the defensive.

  Example: "Is the lunch routine overwhelming?" (rather than, "Bonnie, why is there a lot of crying in your classroom at lunch time?")

- Even if people are not being attentive, do not ask "by name" questions to get their attention or embarrass them for not paying attention. Such actions can cause resentment and further noninvolvement.

- Be careful not to dish out too much praise or respond to participants with words such as, "That's a good question" or "What a great idea." Other staff members not receiving such praise may interpret their questions or responses as being less valued.

Adapted from Martin, C., & Hackett, D. (1993). <u>Facilitation skills for team leaders</u> (pp. 20 - 21). Palo Alto, CA: Crisp Publications.

Active Listening

Essential to encouraging greater participation in group situations is establishing rapport through good listening. This means suppressing the urge to interrupt, finish a speaker's sentence, or chime in as soon as the speaker takes a breath for air. Participants need to feel comfortable "thinking out loud" in a group. Paying attention and employing active listening skills demonstrates respect for the speaker. Indeed, good listening can be a powerful action to encourage greater involvement in decision making.

Active listening, as the term implies, is not a passive activity. It means establishing and maintaining eye contact with the speaker, being tuned in to the nuances of body language, and using nonverbal signals like facing the speaker, smiling, or nodding your head to establish rapport.

Paraphrasing and checking for meaning is another way to help people reach mutual understanding on important issues:

- "Let me see if I understand your position. Are you saying that . . .?"
- "Let me restate your last point to see if I understand you correctly."
- "What I hear you saying is. . . Is that right?"
- "Do you mean that. . .?"

Asking for clarification and expansion of what speakers say also communicates that you value their point of view:

- "Tell me more about that."
- "Could you explain what you mean by. . . ?"

Soliciting Feedback

Inviting staff to suggest ways that procedures can be improved can stimulate creative problem solving and empower people to improve their work environment. When teachers are invited to give feedback, question procedures, suggest alternatives, and exchange differing points of view, they are offered a legitimate way to improve the organization before frustrations take root and cause job complacency or job dissatisfaction. Moderate griping can be healthy, as long as it is channeled toward improving conditions.

One director of a large center awarded a $50 prize for the best suggestion each month. She called it the Big-Idea-of-the-Month Award. When she initiated the award, she emphasized that contributions could be any suggestions for doing something that improved the quality of the center. At the end of each month, she shared the ideas with the entire staff, and together they selected the winner. The creative suggestions submitted by teachers resulted in a new way to code children's books, a different procedure for carpools, a more systematic way to distribute parent newsletters, and a clever contraption to get sand off the children before they came in from the playground. As a result of this single initiative, the director noticed that much of the griping and complaining among the staff disappeared. In their place was a new attitude—a "we-can-solve-that" spirit of school improvement.

E ffective leaders seek first to understand, then to be understood.

Stephen Covey

Remember, though, that the most important kind of feedback you can solicit is informal and is acquired daily. This requires sensitivity to the body language and the nuances of behavior that convey messages about how individuals feel about their work environment. A two-minute chat in the doorway with a teacher can yield powerful information, helping you become more responsive to that teacher's needs.

Balancing Discussion and Dialogue

Understanding the subtle difference between discussion and dialogue can help you and your staff negotiate the difficult terrain of participative management.

- Discussion is a close examination of an issue with an exchange of opinions, sometimes using argument, in an effort to reach agreement.

- Dialogue is an exchange of ideas designed to build mutual understanding. It is a collective inquiry in which we suspend opinions, share openly, and think creatively about difficult issues.

Effective directors know how to balance dialogue and discussion in group meetings. You'll probably find that your staff feel fairly comfortable with discussion skills— they know how to support and defend their opinions. Discussion can be an efficient way to reach a decision in a group. But when a complex decision must be made, when stakes are high and opinions are polarized, discussion has its limitations. Discussion alone often fails to maximize the contributions each staff member can make. It minimizes the learning the group can do together to create new thinking and generate original solutions. Moreover, the decisions that a group arrives at through discussion often mask unresolved conflict.

Balancing dialogue and discussion helps build consensus and improve the quality of decisions. Dialogue requires skills that can be learned and practiced. Dialogue is characterized by

- suspending judgment
- not considering someone with a different point of view as an adversary
- being willing to expose your reasoning and underlying assumptions
- exploring viewpoints more broadly and deeply
- being open to conflicting data

Directors need to encourage the use of dialogue and help staff become less attached to their ideas and positions. As directors become less reliant on persuasion as a means of influencing others, they will achieve reflective openness— a genuine willingness to challenge their own thinking and assumptions and to change their position on an issue.

Brainstorming: Getting the Creative Juices Flowing

Brainstorming is an effective strategy for gathering ideas that can lead to goal setting, problem solving, or action planning. The point of brainstorming a topic is to generate as many different "rough-draft" ideas as possible in a short period of time while suspending the urge to evaluate or come to agreement about a solution.

Brainstorming is valuable because it recognizes that people process information differently. A synergizing effect is generated when one person's idea stimulates a new and different idea in someone else. For brainstorming to be successful, the following rules must be followed:

- keep the group small; 8 to10 participants is ideal
- include nonconventional participants (the janitor, the cook, a parent) for a fresh perspective
- welcome all ideas (even wacky and weird ones)
- stress that contributions should be concise
- encourage "hitchhiking" (building upon others' ideas)
- record all the ideas on flip chart paper and post them for everyone to see during the brainstorming session
- don't discuss or evaluate ideas until the brainstorming is completed

Brainstorming works best when the problem being tackled is fairly narrow and well defined (How do we increase attendance at our annual fundraiser? How can we make drop-off and pick-up less frantic?). It is helpful to let everyone know about the issue prior to the brainstorming session. That way creative ideas can be brewing even before the meeting begins.

The facilitator's role in a brainstorming session is critical in maintaining momentum: "We've come up with six interesting suggestions, let's see if we can generate six more in our remaining time."

The facilitator must be adept at handling any negative or evaluative reactions expressed during the idea-generating phase. Comments like "We've tried that once before," "Sounds too expensive," "We'd never have time to do that," or "The central office would never approve that idea" can stifle creativity. Ringing a loud cowbell or pressing an annoying buzzer when someone offers an evaluative comment or groaning when an absurd idea is tendered are ways to playfully help participants suppress the urge to analyze or judge suggestions too quickly. When this happens, use the opportunity to remind participants of the importance of suspending judgment.

Rough-draft thinking is just like rough-draft writing—it needs encouragement, not evaluation. Many people don't understand this. If they notice a flaw in someone's thinking, they point it out. They think they've been helpful. But rough-draft ideas need to be clarified, researched, and modified before being subjected to critical evaluation. The time of critical evaluation can make the difference between the life and death of a new idea..

Sam Kaner

Do . . .

- keep things rolling at a fast clip.

- encourage people to take turns.

- treat silly ideas the same as serious ideas.

- move around to create a lively feeling.

- reiterate the purpose often: "Who else has a suggestion for increasing parent attendance at our annual fundraiser?"

- expect a second wave of creative ideas after the obvious ones are exhausted.

Don't . . .

- interrupt when someone is offering an idea.

- say, "We've already got that one."

- say, "Hey, you don't really want me to write that one, do you?"

- favor the "best" thinkers.

- use frowns, raised eyebrows, or other nonverbal gestures to signal disapproval.

- start the process without clearly setting the time limit.

- rush or pressure the group. Silence usually means that people are thinking.

Adapted from Kaner, S. (1996). Facilitator's guide to participatory decision-making (p. 101). Gabriola Island, British Columbia: New Society Publishers.

Some directors have experimented with variations in brainstorming techniques to get the creative juices flowing. One method is reverse brainstorming, in which participants present ideas counter to their goal ("What are all the ways we can discourage parents from attending our annual fundraiser?" "How can we make sure our drop-off and pick-up will be really chaotic?"). Sometimes when a group thinks how to make things go wrong, creative solutions for solving difficult problems evolve.

Another way to stimulate right-brain thinking is to have the group think in metaphoric terms about the issue being discussed ("A really successful fundraiser is like a. . ." or "A smooth-functioning arrival and dismissal is like a. . ."). Connecting concrete experiences to metaphoric images frees the brain to think about the essential characteristics of the experience.

Facilitating a brainstorming session is definitely easier if you are comfortable with ambiguity and confusion, because ambiguity and confusion are essential elements in the creative mix of ideas that predominates before some degree of clarity emerges. If by disposition you are linear, precise, and logical in your thinking, you may want to turn over the facilitation role in a brainstorming session to someone who has a higher tolerance for ambiguity and confusion.

©Copyright Ed Arno (Science 80). Reprinted with permission.

Recording Ideas

In most centers participation in meetings is not balanced. A few outspoken teachers do most of the talking while others sit and listen. This norm can be changed when people's ideas are recorded on a flip chart for everyone to see. Documenting your staff's contributions in writing is important for several reasons:

- Committing a person's ideas to paper has the powerful effect of validating the importance of that person's contribution. This encourages people to participate in future meetings.

- Individuals have different learning styles. Many people are visual learners; when they can see an idea in print, they have an easier time understanding and remembering it.

- Recording people's contributions provides a record of what transpired. Memories are notoriously fuzzy. Writing information on a flip chart helps extend the limits of the human brain. Having something in writing can help jog the memory about what happened.

The two most common techniques for recording contributions are using a flip chart during a meeting and writing up and distributing minutes after a meeting. Recording ideas on a flip chart during a meeting creates a group memory. This helps the group focus on issues being discussed and provides an instant record of what was decided and how it was decided. Writing up and distributing minutes after a meeting serves to remind people who said what and how a particular issue was decided. It also serves to keep individuals who missed the meeting informed about what transpired.

Building Consensus

You and your staff can tackle tough issues by using a variety of consensus-building techniques and avoiding other decision-making methods that result in dividing the staff into winners and losers. The aim of consensus building is to help achieve a position that is satisfying to all. Consensus means general agreement. When done right, consensus decision-making strategies reconcile the diverse opinions of staff members and integrate them into a common solution that, many times, was not the original position of any individual or subgroup.

As the facilitator, you cannot control whether consensus results, but you can play an important leadership role by modeling detached attention. Detached attention means simply being open to all combinations of ideas. If you become attached to an idea as the "the right way," your staff will certainly feel it too, and you will undermine the consensus-building process.

N one of us is as smart as all of us.

Peter B. Grazier

Attitudes and Behaviors
Required for Consensus Decision Making

- Ability to speak for oneself—"I prefer," "I need"

- Ability to stay focused on the task and process

- Clear, honest, and direct speech in terms of who, what, when, where

- Ability to restate concerns or requests as suggestions or proposals ("I have trouble with this and would feel better if we added. . .")

- Ability to distinguish fact from opinion

- Low level of defensiveness as people question ideas

- Willingness to listen and consider other viewpoints

- Commitment to finding the best answer

- Ability to listen for and synthesize areas of agreement

- Patience to hold back from premature decision making

Adapted from Harrington-Mackin, D. (1994). The team building toolkit (pp. 110 - 111). New York: American Management Association.

Consensus-building strategies strengthen commitment and promote ownership because *everyone's* opinion is valued. For consensus to exist, it is not necessary for everyone to agree completely, but it is necessary for every member of your staff to be heard and, in the end, agree not to sabotage the final decision. It is not necessary that everyone consider the decision the best one, only that they agree they will give it a try.

Some directors have used finger voting to gauge the strength of commitment to different decisions under consideration. The following table describes this method along with some other consensus-building strategies you might want to try.

Consensus-Building Strategies

- **Finger voting.** Group members hold up fingers to indicate the level of their support.

Five fingers:	Total agreement, best solution, complete support
Four fingers:	Agree, good solution, support
Three fingers:	Okay with me, willing to support
Two fingers:	Don't agree, not my choice, but I can live with it
One finger:	No way, let's think of an alternative

- **Negative voting.** When several solutions to a problem are proposed, ask individuals to indicate which options they could not live with. Eliminate those that are unacceptable, and focus on the choices with the least opposition.

- **Essential features.** Identify the elements of each proposal that the staff agree with. Use these as the basis for generating other agreements, combinations, or acceptable refinements of the original proposals.

- **Criteria matrix.** Develop a matrix of the agreed-upon criteria or necessary conditions that should be present in any decision being made (e.g., the solution should be family friendly, should not have any negative financial consequences on the center, etc.). List these criteria across the top, and list proposed alternatives down the side. Use the matrix as a checklist to see how well each alternative meets the agreed-upon criteria (yes/no or a numerical scale can be used). Then, see how each proposed solution adds up.

- **Plus- and-minus tally.** Write each alternative on a separate sheet of flip chart paper. Staff members can then discuss and list the positive (+) aspects of each proposal and the negative (-) aspects.

- **Rank order.** Have group members write each alternative on a separate slip of paper. Ask them to arrange their slips in order—from most desirable to least desirable. The slips of paper can then be collected and tallied.

- **Dot voting.** Alternatives generated from a group discussion are written on flip chart paper and posted on the wall. Each staff member gets 5 to 8 dot stickers. They can use these dots to "vote" for the ideas listed, even placing more than one sticker next to an item they feel particularly strong about.

- **Straw voting.** This is a variation of dot sticker voting. Distribute five straws to everyone in the group. They can then use these to cast their vote for different ideas under consideration. Half-votes are permitted and it is permissible to cast more than one straw vote for an item.

- **1-2-6 problem solving.** Ask individuals to write down their solutions to a problem on separate slips of paper. Then have them pair up with another individual, share their ideas, and agree on a solution. Combine three pairs, share ideas, and generate a single solution. Ideas from the six-member groups are then shared to generate a solution by the entire group.

- **Pyramid process.** The pyramid process is a variation of the 1-2-6 problem solving technique. It is effective when a group has to come up with a single product, such as writing the center's mission statement. It is best done over several meetings so the group has time to reflect between meetings. At the first meeting, introduce the task and agree on the essential elements of the product (e.g., the mission statement must be fewer than 100 words and focus on children and families). Before the second meeting, have individuals write down phrases or ideas that they want captured in a mission statement. At the second meeting, group people in pairs and have them work on a statement (20 minutes). At a third meeting combine pairs; have the new foursomes develop a statement. At the final meeting share the products of the four-person groupings. Modify, revise, and agree upon a final product.

CHAPTER 9

Avoiding the Pitfalls of Collaboration

Implementing a model of participative management will not be without obstacles. Time pressures, the presence of dominant coalitions, and the potential for blind compliance known as groupthink are some of the pitfalls you may encounter in your effort to make your center more collaborative.

Time Pressures Sometimes Rule Out Collaboration

In early childhood program administration, there are deadlines, mandates, and external pressures that can create a time crunch in making and implementing decisions. Despite your best intentions to involve other people, sometimes it just isn't possible.

To be sure, implementing a model of participative management in your center requires an initial investment of time to reflect on current organizational structures and decision-making processes and to evaluate how changes can improve the center. Simply put, group decisions require more time than do individual decisions. Participation involves discussion, debate, and often conflict. Speed and efficiency are not characteristics of shared decision making.

Remember that collaboration and shared decision making do not mean discussion for its own sake. Participative management is not about setting up extra meetings that take teachers and support staff away from their primary task of working with children and parents. When done right, collaboration involves a certain investment of time by all parties, but involvement should be valuable to participants and lead to greater job satisfaction, commitment, and professional fulfillment.

Controlling Dominant Coalitions

The lack of diversity in a group in terms of background, expertise, and ideology may promote cohesiveness. But if cohesiveness isn't channeled in constructive and positive ways, it may result in the formation of a dominant coalition that will block attempts to implement a model of shared decision making. Dominant coalitions may be formal coalitions (school-age teachers, kindergarten parents, kitchen staff) or informal coalitions (cliques). Some coalitions have more status, power, and influence do than others.

Mixing group membership for different kinds of decisions may help reduce the incidence of a dominant coalition. Strong leadership in group meetings that ensures that less vocal participants have an opportunity to be heard also helps neutralize the impact of a more vocal, outspoken coalition.

Sometimes during a meeting it may be necessary to limit participation by an individual who represents the interests of a dominant coalition. This must be done tactfully and respectfully.

- "Darlene, we appreciate your contribution. However, it might be well to hear from some other teachers now. Would some of you who have not spoken care to add your ideas?"

- "Jeff, you've made several good points, and I am wondering if someone else might like to make some remarks?"

- "Since everyone hasn't had an opportunity to speak yet, Janice, I wonder if you would hold your comments until a little later?"

Preventing Groupthink

Strong cohesiveness can promote uniformity within a group. The problem with uniformity is that it can also produce a like-mindedness that is uncritical. This phenomenon has been referred to as groupthink. Groupthink is a mindset that takes over when the desire for agreement in a group overrides the ability of the group to accurately assess a problem and consider a full range of decision options.

"Well, heck! If all you smart cookies agree, who am I to dissent?"

- **Illusion of invulnerability** – members are overly optimistic and will take unreasonable risks.

- **Collective rationalization** – members explain away warnings contrary to group thinking.

- **Illusion of morality** – members believe their decisions are morally correct.

- **Excessive stereotyping** – members may construct negative stereotypes of others outside the group.

- **Pressure for conformity** – members pressure those in the group who express contrary opinions as being disloyal.

- **Self-censorship** – members who have reservations about the majority opinion withhold dissenting views and counterarguments to promote the appearance of cohesiveness.

- **Illusion of unanimity** – members perceive falsely that everyone agrees; silence is seen as consent.

- **Mindguards** – some members may protect the group from information that could threaten group cohesiveness or their illusion of solidarity.

From Janis, I. L. (1982). Groupthink. Boston: Houghton Mifflin Publishing Company. Reprinted with permission.

To prevent groupthink, it is important to be as neutral as possible when conveying a decision-making task to a group, withholding your preferences and expectations until all participants have fully expressed their opinions. The goal is to foster an air of open inquiry that elicits divergent points of view. Assigning the role of devil's advocate is another way to support the importance of considering all options, even seemingly unpopular alternatives. Most important, allow adequate time for discussing the merits of several options before settling on a particular course of action.

It is better to debate a question without settling it than to settle a question without debating it.

Joseph Joubert

CHAPTER 10

A Final Word

Some people believe that participation in decision making is an either/or proposition—employees are involved or not involved. The framework presented here underscores the point that shared decision making cannot be reduced to such simplistic terms. Where participative management is successful, there are different levels of participation depending on the issues, the people, and the external constraints affecting the program.

Your program is unique, so the way you go about realigning roles and relationships to unleash your staff's creative energy and influence will also be unique. The key is that you have thoughtfully and systematically looked at the "big picture." You know who the key stakeholders are; you know what types of decisions need to be made; and you have carefully weighed the pros and cons of different levels of involvement. There is no pat formula, no quick and easy recipe to follow. You must be committed to the process and you must be willing to take some risks.

Regardless of the setting, directors who embrace a philosophy of participative management uniformly believe that their teachers have the potential to be leaders. They have a deep conviction that programs that tap the knowledge of their staff make more informed decisions, garner higher levels of productivity, and enjoy greater staff morale because of people's increased sense of control and accountability.

It is important to remember, though, that involvement should be viewed as a means to an end and not an end in itself. The goal of participative management is to improve program practices for children and families and the quality of work life for staff. Collaboration and shared decision making do not mean discussion for its own sake. Just because there are more meetings scheduled on the staff calendar does not necessarily mean that people have a greater voice in the direction of the program. Meetings must be substantive; involvement must be genuine.

Participative management

- increases commitment to decisions that are made

- engenders less resistance than other forms of leadership

- increases the psychological ownership of decisions

- promotes better follow-through on decisions

- can lead to higher-quality child care

But it also...

- takes more time

- necessitates more advanced group leadership skills

- requires a willingness by the director to relinquish control and influence over all decisions

L eadership which taps the creativity of those who are at the center of a project . . . will always do better than leadership that uses authority.

Harold Howe, II

A collaborative center should also not be confused with a congenial center. Just because teachers care about one another and enjoy each other's camaraderie, does not necessarily mean that collaborative decision-making processes are in place. To be sure, greater collegiality may be a positive outcome of shared decision making, but it should not be the driving force of your efforts. When co-worker relations reinforce collaborative structures so that teachers engage in reflective practice together and see themselves as partners in a learning organization, then the twin goals of collaboration and collegiality will both be met.

In the end, shared decision making is a delicate balance of meeting both organizational needs and individual needs. If endeavors in participative management are to be successful, cooperation and teamwork require that individuals subordinate their personal preferences to group goals. This is a difficult shift that does not happen overnight. With patience and persistence, however, it is possible to lead your staff to a new way of thinking about their roles and their collective responsibility for shaping organizational excellence.

This book has introduced the theory behind participative management and the tools that can help you increase the circle of influence by inviting the collaboration of your staff. With a commitment to action, you can be the driving force that makes participative management a reality in your center.

When the best leader's work is done, the people say, "We did it ourselves."

Lao-tzu

For Further Reading

Bendaly, L. (1997). *Strength in numbers.* New York: McGraw-Hill Ryerson.

Bloom, P. J. (1996). *Improving the quality of work life in early childhood settings: Resource guide and technical manual for the Early Childhood Work Environment Survey (Rev. ed.).* Wheeling, IL: The Center for Early Childhood Leadership, National-Louis University.

Bloom, P. J., Sheerer, M., & Britz, J. (1991). *Blueprint for action: Achieving center-based change through staff development.* Lake Forest, IL: New Horizons.

Bridges, E. M. (1967). A model for shared decision making in the school principalship. *Educational Administration Quarterly, 3,* 49-61.

Bruno, H. E., & Copeland, M. L. (1999, Spring). Decisions! decisions! Decision making structures which support quality. *Leadership Quest, 3(2),* 6-9.

Carter, M., & Curtis, D. (1998). *Visionary director: A handbook for dreaming, organizing, and improvising in your center.* St. Paul, MN: Redleaf Press.

Conley, S. (1991). Review of research on teacher participation in school decision making. *Review of Research in Education, 17,* 225-266.

Covey, S. (1991). *Principled-centered leadership.* New York: Fireside Books.

Ettinger, J. (1989). *The winning trainer.* Houston, TX: Gulf.

Gelatt, H. B. (1991). *Creative decision making.* Menlo Park, CA: Crisp Publications.

Glickman, C. D. (1985). *Supervision of instruction.* Boston: Allyn & Bacon.

Harrington-Mackin, D. (1994). *The team building toolkit.* New York: American Management Association.

Hewes, D. (1998, November). Decision making: A linear process. *Child Care Information Exchange,* 26-30.

Janis, I. L. (1982). *Groupthink.* Boston: Houghton Mifflin Publishing.

Kaner, S. (1996). *Facilitator's guide to participative decision-making.* Gabriola Island, BC, Canada: New Society Publishers.

Kostelnik, M. J. (1984, August). Real consensus or groupthink? *Child Care Information Exchange,* 25-30.

Martin, C., & Hackett, D. (1993). *Facilitation skills for team leaders.* Palo Alto, CA: Crisp Publications.

Morrison, E. K. (1994). *Leadership skills: Developing volunteers for organizational success.* Tucson, AZ: Fisher Books.

Neugebauer, R. (1983, March/April). Do you have delegation-phobia? *Child Care Information Exchange,* 2-6.

Neugebauer, R. (1982, January). Making decisions. *Child Care Information Exchange,* 17-24.

Pokras, S. (1997). *Working in teams.* Menlo Park, CA: Crisp Publications.

Saphier, J., Bigda-Peyton, T., & Pierson, G. (1989). *How to make decisions that stay made.* Alexandria, VA: Association for Supervision and Curriculum Development.

Scott, J., & Flanigan, E. (1996). *Achieving consensus.* Menlo Park, CA: Crisp Publications.

Smith, S., & Scott, J. (1990). *The collaborative school.* Reston, VA: National Association of Secondary School Principals.

Smylie, M. (1992, Spring). Teacher participation in school decision making: Assessing willingness to participate. *Educational Evaluation and Policy Analysis, 14* (1), 53-67.

Schmuck, R.A., & Runkel, P.J. (1985). *The handbook of organization development in schools.* Palo Alto, CA: Mayfield Publishing.

Wood, C. J. (1984). Participatory decision making: Why doesn't it seem to work? *The Educational Forum, 49*(1), 55-64.

Zeece, P. D. (1998). Power lines—The use and abuse of power in child care programming. In B. Neugebauer & R. Neugebauer (Eds.), *The art of leadership: Managing early childhood organizations* (pp. 29-33). Redmond, WA: Exchange Press.

Appendix A

Appendix B

Appendix C

Decision-Making Influence Questionnaire

This questionnaire has two parts. Part I assesses your perceptions about your current and desired levels of decision-making influence. Part II assesses your perceptions about the way decisions are made at this center. Your honest and candid responses to these questions are appreciated. When you have completed your questionnaire, please put it in the envelope provided and place it in the Questionnaire Return Box in the office. There is no need to include your name.

PART I. Listed below are 50 common organizational decisions and actions. Please indicate (✔) in the space provided, how much influence you *currently have* and how much influence you would *like to have* in each of the areas listed.

TYPE OF ORGANIZATIONAL DECISIONS	CURRENT INFLUENCE			DESIRED INFLUENCE		
	Very little influence	Some influence	Considerable influence	Very little influence	Some influence	Considerable influence
Staff supervision and professional development						
Establish guidelines and procedures for staff orientation						
Establish guidelines for supervision of teaching staff						
Establish guidelines for supervision of support staff						
Determine the type and frequency of in-service training						
Establish career ladder guidelines						
Instructional practices and scheduling						
Determine the daily schedule of classroom activities						
Select instructional materials and equipment						
Determine content of the curriculum						
Determine the type and frequency of special events						
Establish an annual calendar						
Enrollment and grouping						
Determine enrollment criteria and policies						
Determine group size and patterns (e.g., mixed age)						
Determine grouping assignments						
Determine adult-child ratios						
Determine the placement of children with special needs						
Fiscal policies and practices						
Determine tuition and fees						
Determine salaries and benefits						
Set priorities for center and classroom expenditures						
Determine fundraising priorities and goals						
Determine procedures for accounts payable/receivable						
Human resource allocation						
Determine the qualifications for different positions						
Determine staff hiring criteria and procedures						
Determine the staffing pattern and teaching assignments						
Set staff work schedules						
Determine the criteria for promotion and advancement						

TYPE OF ORGANIZATIONAL DECISIONS	CURRENT INFLUENCE			DESIRED INFLUENCE		
	Very little influence	Some influence	Considerable influence	Very little influence	Some influence	Considerable influence
Centerwide goals and educational objectives						
Determine the center's philosophy						
Determine educational objectives for different age groups						
Determine the frequency and scheduling of staff meetings						
Determine staff meeting agendas						
Establish a code of conduct (e.g., dress, confidentiality)						
Parent relations						
Determine who serves as primary contact with parents						
Set expectations for parent involvement						
Determine the format and frequency of parent conferences						
Determine the type and frequency of parent education						
Determine the content of the parent newsletter						
Community relations						
Determine the type of contacts with community agencies						
Establish marketing and public relations priorities						
Determine the content of press releases						
Establish a risk management plan						
Determine the type of contacts with local schools						
Facilities management						
Determine how space is allocated						
Determine how space is arranged						
Establish food service procedures and contracts						
Determine capital improvement priorities						
Determine maintenance procedures and contracts						
Evaluation practices (child, staff, center)						
Determine the type and frequency of child assessments						
Determine guidelines for staff performance appraisals						
Determine type and frequency of programwide evaluations						
Determine center's accreditation timeline and procedures						
Determine the use and distribution of evaluation data						

PART II.   Check (✔) all that describe how decisions are made at this center/school most of the time.

_____ Teachers are asked their opinions on important issues.
_____ The director likes to make most of the decisions.
_____ People don't feel free to express their opinions.
_____ Everyone provides input on the content of staff meetings.
_____ People provide input, but decisions have already been made.
_____ Teachers make decisions about things that directly affect them.
_____ Decisions are made by those who know most about the problem or issue.

What suggestions do you have for promoting shared decision making at this center?

Bloom, P. J. (2000). _Circle of influence: Implementing shared decision making and participative management._ Lake Forest, IL: New Horizons.

Scoring Key for
Decision-Making Influence Questionnaire

Part I

1. Compute the scores for current decision-making influence for each person using the following point value:

    - very little influence = 0
    - some influence = 1
    - considerable influence = 2

Current decision-making scores will range from 0 to 100 points.

2. Compute the scores for desired decision-making influence for each person using the same point value as above. Scores will range from 0 to 100.

3. Add together all the staff's current decision-making influence scores and divide by the total number of staff to get an average current decision-making influence score.

4. Add together all the staff's desired decision-making influence scores and divide by the total number of staff to get an average desired decision-making influence score.

5. Subtract the average current decision-making influence score from the average desired decision-making influence score to get a decision-making discrepancy score.

Part II

1. Tally the number of individuals on your staff who checked the first item.

2. Divide that number by the total number of individuals completing the questionnaire. This figure represents the percentage of staff who believe that the first statement characterizes decision-making processes at your center.

3. Follow this same procedure for the remaining six items to yield the percentage of staff who agree with each of the items.

Decision-Making Blueprint for Best Care Child Development Center

	D	AB	CC	LT	T	AT	PC
Staff supervision and professional development							
Establish guidelines and procedures for staff orientation	■	●	●	●	●	●	●
Establish guidelines for supervision of teaching staff	■	●	●	●	●	✳	✳
Establish guidelines for supervision of support staff	■	●	✳	✳	✳	✳	✳
Determine the type and frequency of in-service training	▲	✳	▲	▲	●	●	●
Establish career ladder guidelines	■	●	●	●	●	✳	✳
Instructional practices and scheduling							
Determine the daily schedule of classroom activities	●	✳	▲	▲	●	●	✳
Select instructional materials and equipment	●	✳	■	●	●	●	✳
Determine the content of the curriculum	●	●	■	●	●	●	✳
Determine the type and frequency of special events	▲	▲	●	●	●	●	▲
Establish an annual calendar	▲	▲	●	●	●	●	●
Enrollment and grouping							
Determine enrollment criteria and policies	■	●	●	●	✳	✳	✳
Determine group size and patterns (e.g., mixed age)	■	●	●	●	✳	✳	✳
Determine grouping assignments	●	●	▲	▲	●	●	✳
Determine adult-child ratios	■	●	●	●	●	✳	✳
Determine the placement of children with special needs	●	✳	▲	▲	●	●	✳
Fiscal policies and practices							
Determine tuition and fees	▲	▲	✳	✳	✳	✳	✳
Determine salaries and benefits	■	●	●	●	●	●	●
Set priorities for center and classroom expenditures	■	●	●	●	●	●	●
Determine fundraising priorities and goals	●	■	✳	✳	✳	✳	●
Determine procedures for accounts payable/receivable	■	●					
Human resource allocation							
Determine the qualifications for different positions	▲	✳	▲	▲	✳	✳	▲
Determine staff hiring criteria and procedures	■	✳	●	●	✳	✳	✳
Determine the staffing pattern and teaching assignments	■	✳	●	●	●	✳	✳
Set staff work schedules	■		●	●	●	●	●
Determine the criteria for promotion and advancement	■	●	●	●	●	✳	●
Centerwide goals and educational objectives							
Determine the center's philosophy	▲	▲	▲	▲	●	●	▲
Determine educational objectives for different age groups	▲	●	▲	▲	●	●	●
Determine the frequency and scheduling of staff meetings	■	●	●	●	●	●	●
Determine staff meeting agendas	▲		▲	▲	●	●	●
Establish a code of conduct (e.g., dress, confidentiality)	▲	▲	▲	▲	●	●	▲
Parent relations							
Determine who serves as primary contact with parents	▲	●	●	●	✳	✳	▲
Set expectations for parent involvement	▲	●	●	●	●	✳	▲
Determine the format and frequency of parent conferences	▲	●	●	●	●	✳	▲
Determine the type and frequency of parent education	●	●	●	●	✳	✳	■
Determine the content of the parent newsletter	●	●	●	●	●	●	■

	D	AB	CC	LT	T	AT	PC
Community relations							
Determine the type of contacts with community agencies	■	●	✳	✳			●
Establish marketing and public relations priorities	■	●	✳	✳			●
Determine the content of press releases	■	●	✳	✳			●
Establish a risk management plan	■	●	✳	✳			
Determine the type of contacts with local schools	■	●	●	●	✳		●
Facilities management							
Determine how space is allocated	■	●	●	●	●	✳	✳
Determine how space is arranged	▲		▲	▲	●	●	
Establish food service procedures and contracts	■	●	●	●	✳	✳	
Determine capital improvement priorities	■	●	●	●	✳	✳	✳
Determine maintenance procedures and contracts	■	●	●	●	✳	✳	
Evaluation practices (child, staff, center)							
Determine the type and frequency of child assessments	▲	▲	▲	▲	●	●	✳
Determine guidelines for staff performance appraisals	■	●	●	●	●	●	●
Determine type and frequency of programwide evaluations	■	●	●	●	●	●	●
Determine center's accreditation timeline and procedures	■	●	●	●	●	✳	●
Determine the use and distribution of evaluation data	■	●	●	●	✳		●

D = Director
AB = Advisory Board
CC = Curriculum Coordinator
LT = Lead Teachers
T = Teachers
AT = Assistant Teachers
PC = Parent Coordinator

■ = Responsible for final decision
● = Provide input on the decision
▲ = Share jointly in making the decision
✳ = Be informed about the decision

NOTES

Available from New Horizons

The Director's Toolbox: A Management Series for Early Childhood Administrators

- *Circle of Influence: Implementing Shared Decision Making and Participative Management* $14.95

- *Making the Most of Meetings: A Practical Guide* $14.95 (available August 2000)

- *Leadership in Action: How Effective Directors Get Things Done* $14.95 (available December 2000)

A Trainer's Guide is also available for each topic in the Director's Toolbox Series. Each guide provides step-by-step instructions for planning and presenting a dynamic and informative six-hour workshop. Included are trainers' notes and presentation tips, instructions for conducting learning activities, reproducible handouts, and transparencies. $49.95

Other books by Paula Jorde Bloom

- *Avoiding Burnout: Strategies for Managing Time, Space, and People in Early Childhood Education* $14.95

- *A Great Place to Work: Improving Conditions for Staff in Young Children's Programs* $6.00

- *Blueprint for Action: Achieving Center-Based Change Through Staff Development* $28.95

- *Blueprint for Action: Assessment Tools Packet* $11.95

- *Workshop Essentials: A Guide to Planning and Presenting Dynamic Workshops* $14.95 (available March 2000)

To place your order or receive additional information on quantity discounts, contact:

NEW HORIZONS

P.O. Box 863
Lake Forest, Illinois 60045-0863
(847) 295-8131